EVE BROENLAND

COGNITIVE CAPACITY

MAXIMISE YOUR PRODUCTIVITY AND MENTAL BANDWIDTH IN AN OVERLOADED WORLD

To Frank

Your never-ending support makes me love you more every day.

Contents

Definitions

Words matter.

Cognition comes from the Latin *cognoscere*, meaning "to know" or "to become acquainted with". At its root, it is about the act of knowing—the processes by which we take in information, interpret it, store it, recall it, and use it. Cognition is not a single function; it is an orchestra of mental processes: attention, memory, reasoning, language, and problem-solving. When psychologists talk about "cognitive load" or "cognitive bias," they are speaking about the ways this orchestra plays—sometimes in harmony, sometimes in discord.

For our purposes, cognition is not a clinical term. It is the everyday process of being able to think clearly, make sense of a messy and overloaded world, and act with intention. It is the clarity behind a decision, the focus that lets you bring something from thought into reality; the action you bring forth from that thought.

Capacity has a different lineage. The word comes from the Latin *capacitas*, derived from capax, meaning "capable of holding much". At its core, capacity is about containment: how much a vessel can carry. Over time, the word has evolved from describing physical volume—the size of a cup, the seating of a theatre—to describing human potential: our mental capacity, emotional capacity, capacity for work, and capacity for compassion.

Capacity is not static. A glass has a fixed volume, but human beings are more fluid in their nature. Capacity stretches and contracts. It depends on context, on rest and fatigue, on support and stress. You may feel abundant capacity one morning and hollowed out by afternoon. That fluctuation is not failure; it is human.

When we put these two words together—cognition and capacity—we arrive at the central idea of this book. Cognitive capacity is not about cramming more into your mind. It is about recognising that the "vessel" of your attention and energy has limits, and learning how to work with those limits wisely. It is about understanding the mechanics of knowing, and then creating the conditions where your mind has the space to do its best work.

The etymology here matters because it reminds us that how we function in our world is not a simple input-output equation.

Your interaction with the world you live and work in is about the transition between what you perceive, combine that with what you know, how you think, and how much you can hold. The concept of cognitive capacity is a powerful tool for understanding and enhancing our lives. It is a reminder that we are not passive vessels but active conductors of our mental orchestra. We can direct our attention, memory, and energy to operate effectively with and within our surroundings. We can be much more in control, rather than let our overloaded world overwhelm us.

This book will guide you through the challenges we face in relation to cognitive capacity as we navigate every day through a surplus of data, information, communication, and noise. I will provide strategies to manage your capacity, enabling you to be much more productive without the mental exhaustion. The pages that follow will delve into the intricate world of cognition and capacity, offering a practical guide to overcoming information overload.

That is what this book is about: creating cognitive capacity so you can think, decide, create, and live with clarity.

Cognitive capacity is your brain's available mental bandwidth—the total amount of mental resources you have to process information, make decisions, and get things done without becoming overwhelmed. So if you want to become more efficient at processing information, making decisions, or improving your productivity, without the overwhelm, you're in the right place.

Foreword

You're not failing. You're overloaded.

This is the sole reason for me writing this book. It hurts me to read those words. It is something I wish for no one else to feel. Yet, I know it to be true. I know that there are many like you and me who feel they are failing; not doing a good enough job, in work and in life. And it has a massive impact on how we feel about ourselves. It has affected me too. And for that reason, I want to help you.

Back in my days as an environmental manager, as I was working in the mining industry in Perth, Western Australia, I was struggling. I definitely put high expectations on myself, yet I felt I was not meeting the mark. I forced my way through managing the overwhelm I felt, pretty much every day. Some moments were okay or manageable; most were not. I would sometimes even cry on my way to work. Through my challenges of feeling that it was all too much (I described that journey in detail in my book, *Unclogging*), of too much input, too many requests, and too many expectations I put on myself, I realised I needed to learn how to let go. But as I continued on my journey of figuring out what works for me, I realised how much our environment impacts us. Learning that we can't cope with this much input was for me the trigger to help others with this. Because we are overloaded, and for that, we suffer. But that doesn't mean we're failing.

The shift wasn't a sudden epiphany but rather a gradual increase in understanding. It wasn't about acquiring some new productivity hack or downloading a fancy app. It was about recognising the combination of time, tasks, energy, and most importantly, my mental state. Only when I started to consider all of those elements are important to how we perform did my old understanding of input equals output start to crumble. It was like finally seeing the whole picture, instead of just focusing on a single, narrow line. My environmental science background must have come into play here—really seeing the interconnections, but also that we need to know how to operate effectively in our own environment. And that this is possible. The old playbook—that relentless pursuit of efficiency alone—simply wasn't equipped to navigate the complexity of our current world. It was a sense of relief to finally understand that my struggles weren't a sign of failure but rather a testament to the limitations of a fundamentally flawed approach.

My struggles, and perhaps yours, too, stemmed from an unsustainable workload and unrealistic self-expectations. The constant pressure led to emotional distress and near-constant overwhelm. This realisation, however, became a turning point. I understood that my feelings weren't personal failings but a consequence of systemic overload, not necessarily work overload, but also all the other things we try to manage and deal with every day. This insight led me to develop strategies for managing workload and expectations, which I share to help others avoid the same mistake. Because there had to be a better way (and there is!).

If you don't have cognitive capacity, you're not fully there, not 100%. You might sit in the meeting, nodding along, but part of you is elsewhere—half-remembering an unfinished task, half-dreading the next request. You might say yes to a colleague, but inside you're already wondering how on earth you'll fit it in. You overcommit because you feel you have to, and in trying to do it all, you end up doing it poorly. And then the guilt compounds—the inner voice that whispers you're not doing enough, not good enough, not strong enough.

But the truth is, this isn't weakness. It isn't failure. It's what happens when the load exceeds the limit of the system. No one blames a computer for freezing when too many programs are running. No one blames a bridge for buckling under more weight than it was ever designed to bear. And yet, we regularly blame ourselves for not holding up under conditions that are, in fact, unmanageable.

That's why this book exists. Not to hand you another trick for squeezing more into your day, but to remind you that your mind is not broken, your effort is not lacking, and your value is not defined by output alone. We live in a world of relentless input. Cognitive capacity is about you working towards a better balance of interacting with your world. Not overloaded, overworked, or overwhelmed, but focused, clear, and intentional.

When I look back on my own story—those mornings in Perth when I cried in the train before walking into the office—I can see now what I couldn't then: that my exhaustion was not a personal weakness but a predictable outcome of systemic overload. The workload, the requests, and my own expectations—it wasn't that I wasn't capable, it was that the system was demanding more than anyone could sustainably give. And yet I was assuming that we could.

That doesn't mean we can stand back and just blame our overloaded, complex world and our limitations. Absolutely not. This is a case that allows you to truly understand the role you play in this interaction of operating within your environment. That you take accountability for effective information processing, decision-making, and your productivity. The more you get to understand about what's happening beyond the surface (the external part of input is not the same as the internal), the more you'll be able to take control, and that will make all the difference.

And that is the same shift I want for you. Because when you lack cognitive capacity, life narrows. You survive but don't thrive. You show up in body, but not in spirit. But when you protect and expand that capacity, you reclaim something precious: the ability to be present, to give your best without burning out, to live and work with both purpose and peace.

That is what I wish for you.

Then my invitation to you is this: be open and okay to try. That's really all I'm asking of you. Test what suits you—in your workplace, with your preferences, in the works of your life. Think of it like trying on a new outfit: does it fit, does it feel comfortable, and does it make sense for the occasion you're in? Some aspects of this book will feel as though they were tailored just for you. Others may feel awkward, unnecessary, or simply not your style. And that's fine.

The potential of what this book can bring you is not in applying everything word for word. It's in experimenting. It's in noticing what shifts your day, what alleviates your load, what helps you breathe a little more easily. It's in choosing your own perfect fit.

So I invite you to treat these ideas as options, not obligations. Test them. Keep what resonates. Set aside what doesn't. Come back later if something feels more relevant down the track. Your work environment, your role, and the demands of your life—all of these will influence what's useful to you. You are allowed to adapt. In fact, I hope you do.

And here's the beautiful truth: This book's potential depends entirely on your participation. Not your perfection, not your discipline, not your ability to follow instructions to the letter. Just your willingness to engage, to explore, to pay attention to what helps. That's it. You do you.

And the ugly truth: the hardest thing for me in writing a book about information overload is not overloading you. I've tried to keep things clear, practical, and grounded. But we both know the temptation in books like these is to turn them into yet another mountain of "shoulds". And that is the last thing I want for you.

So, can we make an agreement? You do what's best for you. Take what serves you and leave the rest. I give you full permission to skip, to pause, to reread, or to walk away and try again later. You don't owe this book anything. What you do owe yourself is space—the space to discover how you work best, the space to reclaim your clarity, the space to make your capacity manageable again. If this book can help you find even a little more of that space, then it has done its job.

So let's begin with curiosity rather than pressure (you already have enough of that anyway). You may be surprised at how much lighter life feels when you give yourself permission to work with your mind, not against it. Have fun!

PART I

UNDERSTANDING COGNITIVE CAPACITY

CHAPTER 1

WHY CAPACITY MATTERS

Beware the barrenness of a busy life.

— SOCRATES

There is a particular kind of exhaustion that doesn't come from lifting weights or running too far, but from living at full tilt with no margin. You might recognise it. You reach the end of the week having raced through countless emails, sat in back-to-back meetings, cleared your inbox more than once (or didn't even get a chance to do so), and ticked tasks off every list. And yet, despite all that motion, you feel strangely underwhelmed by your own progress. You are tired, but not in the satisfying way that comes after a long hike or a good day's work. It feels more empty—drained but not fulfilled.

A client of mine once showed me his calendar with pride. "Look," he said, "not a single gap. My day is that efficient." It was true. Every slot was booked, sometimes double-booked, with meetings, calls, deadlines, and deliverables. He was running his days like a high-speed train schedule, perfectly timed and always on track. But when I asked him how he felt, he hesitated. Then he admitted something that stayed with me: "I'm here in all these meetings, but half the time I don't even feel present. It's like I'm running to keep up with my own life."

That is the paradox of modern work. We equate full calendars with full lives, busyness with productivity, and motion with meaning. But what actually determines how much we can give to our work, our families, and ourselves isn't the number of hours in a day. It's the amount of capacity we carry within those hours.

Time is fixed. Capacity is variable.

And that difference changes everything.

Think of it this way: Time is the container; capacity is the power source. You can open your calendar and see blocks of availability, but those slots don't guarantee the energy, clarity, or mental sharpness you require to fill them well. It's like heading out on a long drive with your phone at 3% battery. You may still have the app for navigation, but not enough power to use it for long. We understand that with devices, yet we miss it in ourselves.

Time is fixed. Capacity
is variable. And that
difference changes
everything.

The truth is that our minds and bodies are not booking systems. They are more like batteries, running on a limited charge. Push too hard, too often, and the battery depletes faster than you can recharge it. This is why, on some days, you finish a single meaningful task and feel satisfied, while on other days, you rush through dozens and feel empty. The measure isn't the number of hours or tasks. It's the state of your capacity.

Our Cognitive Capacity Is Challenged

Nothing in life is as important as you think it is while you are thinking about it.

—Daniel Kahneman

Psychologists have long recognised that we often underestimate the true demands of work. Daniel Kahneman and Amos Tversky named it the planning fallacy—our persistent tendency to underestimate how long tasks will take, even when experience should make us wiser. The fallacy isn't simply about optimism, though that plays a part. It is about a structural blind spot in the way the human brain models the future. We imagine the smooth, best-case scenario and discount all the small but inevitable frictions: the printer that jams, the colleague who calls, the extra layer of approval, or the moment when our concentration dips.

Kahneman himself admitted, after decades of studying the phenomenon, that even he still falls prey to it. Knowing it exists doesn't seem to protect us against it. Our internal "battery" dictates productivity, not sheer willpower. Ignoring this can lead to burnout. This planning fallacy explains why we consistently underestimate task completion times; unforeseen obstacles always arise. Therefore, understanding our mental capacity is key to effective productivity, paving the way for a more realistic approach. It's the reason projects so often overrun deadlines and why "just a quick email" expands into an hour lost. The fallacy isn't about optimism so much as it is about the brain's blind spot: we imagine best-case scenarios and discount friction, complexity, or interruptions.

Sophie Leroy's research adds another layer with the concept of attention residue, which we'll cover further later on. Each time you switch tasks, your mind doesn't make a clean break. A portion of your attention clings to the previous activity, still replaying fragments of thought. That residue clutters the workspace of your brain, weakening the quality of focus you can bring to the next task. It's like trying to cook dinner while the remnants of breakfast still litter the counter—possible, but messy and less efficient.

Overlaying these two forces is another invisible drain: decision fatigue. Every choice we make—whether to respond now or later, whether to rephrase an email, whether to tackle task A or B—draws on a finite pool of mental energy. Research by Roy Baumeister and colleagues showed that as the day wears on, our decision-making capacity declines. Judges, for instance, were more likely to grant parole early in the day, and less likely just before lunch, when their mental resources were depleted. Most of us aren't sentencing people in court, but we face hundreds of micro-decisions daily: What to prioritise? How to phrase a message? When to say yes or no? The sheer volume quietly exhausts us, leaving us more prone to shortcuts, errors, and reactive thinking.

Combined, these forces form a triple bind. The planning fallacy lures us into overcommitment, attention residue scatters our focus, and decision fatigue erodes our judgment as we navigate the day. We miscalculate, we fragment, and we wear down. And then, ironically, we blame ourselves for being "distracted" or "unproductive," when in fact we are wrestling with structural limits of the human mind. The result is that capacity runs out much sooner than our calendars or to-do lists suggest.

If you've ever reached three o'clock in the afternoon staring blankly at your screen, wondering why you can't focus even though you still technically "have time," this is why. It's not a moral failing. It's a capacity issue.

Books like Cal Newport's *Deep Work* and *A World Without Email* warn us of the same danger from another angle. Work that matters most—the kind that moves projects forward, makes decisions clear, sparks creativity, and builds trust with colleagues—requires stretches of uninterrupted attention. Yet our systems and tools are designed for interruption. Our workplace is a constant source of distraction, and we are constantly bombarded with a lot of noise. Newport's point is that email and instant messaging, for all their convenience, have created an environment in which depth has become the exception rather than the rule.

In Johann Hari's *Stolen Focus*, the angle is even wider: we live in a world optimised for distraction. Every device, every platform, and every app is built to harvest attention, not protect it. The economy doesn't reward calm or depth; it rewards clicks, swipes, and scrolling minutes. Notifications are not neutral—they are engineered interruptions, designed to create just enough urgency that you feel compelled to respond. Hari describes how Silicon Valley's most profitable innovations are not in productivity tools or creativity enhancers but in attention capture. Infinite scroll, autoplay, read receipts, and push alerts—each was developed to extend engagement time, to keep eyes on screens a little longer. It is not an accident that people describe themselves as "addicted" to their phones; platforms are modelled explicitly on the mechanics of slot machines, triggering dopamine spikes that hook behaviour.

The consequence is not just individual distraction but a collective erosion of focus. All those interruptions have an impact on us. When every environment—from workspaces to classrooms to dinner tables—is infiltrated by buzzing devices, attention becomes fragmented as the cultural norm. Deep work feels abnormal, even antisocial, in a culture where the expectation is constant availability. We apologise when we put our phone away rather than when we check it mid-conversation.

What Hari highlights is that the blame does not rest solely on individuals. We are not simply failing to be disciplined enough; we are swimming against systems that have been intentionally constructed to fracture focus. In such a culture, protecting attention requires more than willpower. It requires resistance—sometimes in small gestures, such as leaving the phone in another room, and sometimes in larger movements, like rethinking how workplaces, schools, and families establish their norms.

The sobering insight is this: distraction is no longer a mere side effect of modern life. It has become the norm. And without deliberate countermeasures and putting our own strategies in place, our cognitive capacity quietly fades away, not necessarily by our own fault, but by design. And the evidence stacks up. The more fragmented our attention, the less value we can truly deliver. And the more time we spend confusing activity with progress, the more drained and dissatisfied we feel.

How We See the World

We don't see things as they are, we see them as we are.

—Anaïs Nin

There's another layer too, deeper beneath the surface. Capacity is not just about what we do, but also about how our minds perceive the world. They have to filter the input of data, coming in through our senses, and then our minds define our perception. We like to believe our brains work as solid containers, resulting in our perception of reality. In truth, they are colanders. Information streams in, but only some of it makes it through. What passes through depends on our experiences, our expectations, our fears, and our incentives.

This defines how we see the world.

I once sat in a strategy session with a state finance team that had spent months working on what they thought was a shared project. In reality, they were walking three different paths. One leader filtered for risk, another for opportunity, and another for compliance. They had been in the same meetings, reading the same documents, but interpreting them through different filters. The breakthrough came when they realised that their conflict wasn't about facts but about perspectives. Once they saw that they all had a different perspective, they stopped talking past each other and began to design decisions that accounted for all three.

The more fragmented our
attention, the less value
we can truly deliver. And
the more time we spend
confusing activity with
progress, the more drained
and dissatisfied we feel.

Cognitive psychology has a precise language for what happens when we try to process the firehose of modern input. Schemas are one example—mental frameworks that act like filing systems. They help us interpret new information quickly by slotting it into categories we already understand. When you see a dog for the first time, you don't just register a four-legged creature; you place it in your "animal" schema, connected to ideas of pets, safety, or danger depending on your prior experience. Schemas are efficient, but they're not neutral. They simplify reality, often in ways that miss detail or nuance.

Daniel Levitin, in *The Organized Mind*, points out that modern information flows overwhelm systems designed for scarcity. For most of human history, signals were sparse. A rustle in the bushes might have meant predator or prey. A change in the weather might have meant seeking shelter or moving camp. The human attentional system evolved in this environment of limited, high-stakes input. Our brains are exquisitely adept at filtering out what matters from a small field of competing signals. But today, those signals are no longer scarce—they are endless. The average knowledge worker processes hundreds of emails, chat messages, and notifications each day. Even leisure is saturated with stimulation: podcasts on the commute, endless scrolls of headlines, and autoplay videos. The "limited signals" our brains were designed for have become a never-ending flood of data. Instead of sharpening our focus, the abundance of input splinters it.

Adam Gazzaley and Larry Rosen's *The Distracted Mind* puts it starkly: the brain is not wired for the digital deluge. Their research shows that what we often frame as a problem of "self-control" is in fact a mismatch between ancient neural hardware and modern demands. The prefrontal cortex—responsible for planning, prioritising, and goal maintenance—simply cannot keep pace with the rate at which digital environments present new information. Each alert, each notification, and each fragment of novelty hijacks attention because novelty detection was once a survival mechanism. A new sound in the forest could mean food—or danger. In today's world, it just means another distraction.

Then there are biases. Researchers have catalogued well over 180 of them, each one a predictable distortion in how we process the world. Confirmation bias steers us toward evidence that supports what we already believe. Availability bias causes us to overestimate risks or events that are most vivid in our memory, such as plane crashes or recent headlines. Anchoring bias means the first number we see—whether it's a salary offer or a discount price—skews our judgment far more than it should. These shortcuts evolved to help us decide quickly under pressure, but in a modern workplace saturated with information, they often lead us astray. These cognitive biases significantly impact decision-making, hindering objective analysis. They subtly shape our perceptions, influencing everything from hiring decisions to corporate strategies to how we respond to emails. This inherent human fallibility of having a skewed perspective creates our challenge, as we are constantly overloaded.

Our brains, wired for efficiency, rely on these ingrained biases, leading to flawed interpretations. This impacts our ability to process information objectively. Consequently, crucial details are missed, leading to poor judgment calls and potentially damaging decisions. Overcoming these biases requires conscious effort and critical thinking. This constant battle against cognitive limitations further complicates decision-making in our information-rich world, highlighting the need for improved awareness and effective strategies to mitigate these effects.

And finally, neuroscience brings us back to the architecture of the human brain itself. Our neural wiring did not evolve in boardrooms or inboxes. It was honed over millennia for survival: to detect threats, to respond swiftly, to make "good enough" judgments in the face of uncertainty. Speed and efficiency were rewarded far more than nuance or accuracy. That's why our brains leap to conclusions, why we sometimes react before we reflect, and why calm deliberation often feels like swimming upstream.

The costs are not trivial. Cognitive strain rises because the brain must constantly toggle between streams, a process that burns energy and leaves behind attention residue from unfinished tasks. Working memory overloads because the mental scratchpad is cluttered with fragments of emails, tasks, and half-formed reminders. Decision quality declines, not because we suddenly became careless, but because the sheer weight of competing signals makes it harder to keep long-term goals in mind. The result is a cycle of mental fatigue, poorer judgment, and declining productivity, even as the hours spent "working" increase.

This isn't just theory. Studies have shown that interruptions— even brief ones—can double the number of errors we make. Neuroscientists have measured how constant toggling reduces deep encoding in memory, leaving us with fragments rather than understanding. And workplace surveys reveal that employees increasingly describe themselves as "always busy, rarely effective"—a paradox that reflects precisely this mismatch between biology and environment.

Combined, schemas, biases, and neural shortcuts reveal why, under the strain of overload, we so often default to shallow, reactive, or mistaken responses. The point is not that the mind is broken. It is that the mind is human. And when we ignore that humanity, treating ourselves like endless processors, capacity leaks away.

In short, we are trying to run 21st-century lives on a Paleolithic level of attention. The hardware hasn't caught up. And until we design systems—both technological and personal—that acknowledge these limits, the overload will continue to erode our clarity and our capacity.

The Whole Picture of Productivity

Productivity is less about what you do with your time and more about how you run your mind.

—**ROBIN SHARMA**

Which brings us to the fuller picture of productivity. For too long, the conversation of productivity improvement techniques and strategies has revolved around two levers: time and tasks. They are visible, easy to measure, and simple to discuss. But they are only half of the story. Below the surface sit two more levers: your energy and your mind. Invisible to others, harder to measure, but vital to sustain the visible. Together, these four form a whole: time, task, energy, and mind. When they are in balance, productivity almost feels effortless. When they are out of sync, work feels like grit.

If you look at the model, you'll see four main elements circling around the word productivity. Two sit above the surface, two sit below. This is deliberate. Above the surface are the things most people already think of when they hear the word productivity: time management and task management. These are visible, measurable, and easy to track. You can show someone your calendar. You can share your task list. These tools matter—they bring order and coordination to our days. But they are only half the story. Below the surface are the quieter drivers: energy management and mind management. These are less visible to others, often even to ourselves, but they determine how much of our time and task efforts actually convert into results. Energy is about your physical vitality, your emotional tone, and your ability to sustain engagement. Mind is about your clarity, focus, memory, and mental filters. Together, they shape whether the time and task tools above the surface can actually work.

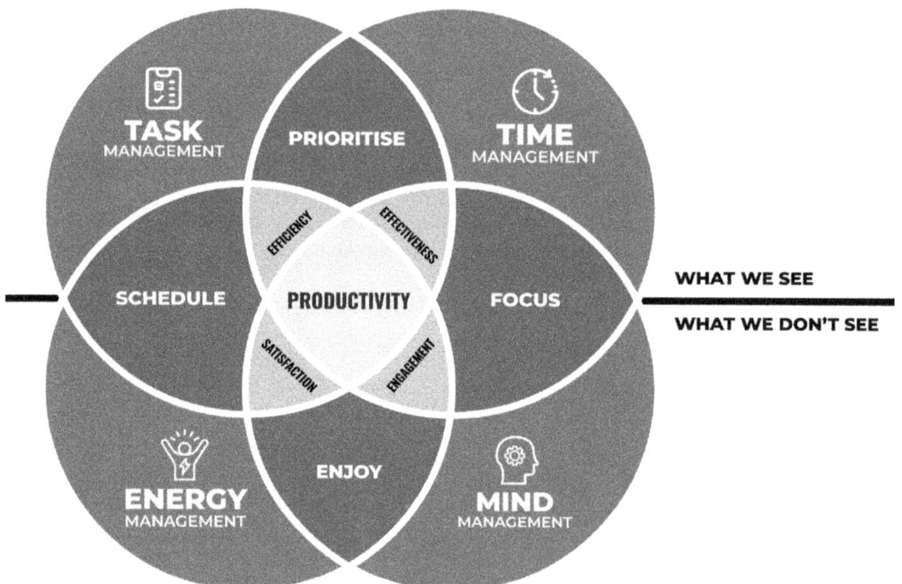

Not taking into account what is below the line, what we don't see, is what is missing from our objective to enhance our productivity. I learned this lesson the hard way in my own career.

As an environmental manager, and perhaps being Dutch played a big part too, I took pride in my efficiency. I streamlined tasks, packed my schedule, and I hate double-handling. Yet no matter how efficient I became, the feeling of overwhelm persisted. What finally changed was that shift in perspective. I stopped trying to outpace overload with efficiency and began to pay attention to what was happening beneath the surface. Energy. Mind. The way I framed my work. The way I filtered everything that came my way: how I channelled my attention. Once I saw productivity as a system, not just a schedule, I could see how my approach led me to not being able to cope.

The more I worked with leaders and professionals across industries, the clearer it became that this broader definition of productivity was not optional. It was the missing link. Everyone was trying to win the race with the same two elements—time and tasks. They were running faster, squeezing harder, and filling every gap. Burning the candle at both ends. But capacity kept collapsing underneath because the invisible levers weren't part of the design. This is why people can spend an entire week in meetings, juggling projects, and answering hundreds of emails, yet still feel empty at the end of it all. They were productive on the surface; however, without energy and mind beneath, the system didn't hold. That's why I divide the model into the line above the surface and the line below the surface. We are used to managing what we ourselves and others can see: meetings, deadlines, and tasks. But the invisible layers—your energy and your mind—are where capacity is won or lost. It is below the surface that real productivity takes root.

At the centre of the model sit four experiences that connect all four core elements: prioritise, schedule, focus, and enjoy.

When all four elements are in play, productivity feels smooth, balanced, and effective. You are in control, and you enjoy what you do. When one element dominates, the system tilts. A calendar full of tasks but no energy beneath it leads to burnout. Energy without time structure leads to aimless drift. Tasks without focus scatter into fragments. Focus without enjoyment becomes brittle.

- **Prioritising** connects task management with time management. Prioritising means choosing what matters most. It's not just about listing tasks but aligning them with the time you have available. Without prioritisation, your list becomes endless and overwhelming and unachievable. With it, you make deliberate trade-offs, putting first things first so your time is invested where it has the greatest impact.

- **Scheduling** connects task management with energy management. Scheduling is more than filling a calendar —it's matching the right task to the right energy. Some work requires sharpness, some patience, some creativity. By scheduling in line with your natural energy rhythms, you avoid wasting your best hours on low-value work and protect yourself from burnout.

- **Focusing** connects time management with mind management. Focus is the discipline of giving your full attention to one thing at a time. It links how you use your hours with how you direct your thoughts. Without focus, time slips away in distractions and multitasking. With focus, your work gains depth, clarity, and momentum.

- **Enjoying** connects energy management with mind management. Enjoying is the often overlooked side of productivity. It's the spark that comes when your mind is engaged and your energy feels aligned. When you enjoy what you do, your satisfaction grows, motivation renews, and productivity becomes sustainable. Enjoyment isn't a luxury —it's fuel.

This model visually represents what is missing in our search for productivity, efficiency, and effectiveness. We focus only, or at least for the majority, on what's above the surface, what's visible, what's tangible, and what's right in front of us. But we have to see the whole picture: productivity is not a two-dimensional equation of time and tasks. It is a four-part system, rooted in both the visible and the invisible, sustained not just by doing but by being.

The Energy You Bring

Energy, not time, is the fundamental currency of high performance.

—Jim Loehr & Tony Schwartz

In my sessions around productivity, I often ask professionals to picture a garden. If you measure productivity only by how many seeds you scatter in the soil, you'll feel busy but not see much growth. Real productivity comes from choosing what to plant, tending to it, spacing it, watering it, and allowing it sunlight and time. It's a balance of effort and attention. Scatter too many seeds and the soil is overwhelmed; pull at every weed and you have no time to nourish. In the same way, the capacity to thrive at work is about more than sowing tasks. It's about tending to the soil of your energy and the climate of your mind.

This way of thinking may feel unusual because the dominant story about productivity has been shaped by industrial metaphors. The factory. The assembly line. Inputs and outputs. These metaphors worked for machines, but they are disastrous for humans. Unlike machines, we are not designed to operate continuously at a constant speed for twenty-four hours a day. We oscillate. We surge, we dip, and we need rest. And unlike machines, we are not interchangeable parts. Each of us brings a unique configuration of filters, experiences, rhythms, and values that shape how we use our capacity. I, for one, have been looking exclusively at my productivity output for way too long; I now know there's much more nuance to it and that it's my job to look at it as a whole, well-functioning ecosystem—like a garden.

Ignoring those differences leads to what Sendhil Mullainathan and Eldar Shafir called tunnelling in their book *Scarcity*. When our capacity is compressed, we don't see the whole picture. We narrow in on what is urgent and visible, often at the expense of what is important and longer-term. Their research shows that scarcity isn't limited to money, although it is most evident in that context. A person short on funds becomes consumed by the next bill, the next expense, and the immediate hole to be patched—leaving little room to think about long-term savings or healthier trade-offs. But the same mechanism applies to time scarcity, attention scarcity, and mental load. When we feel stretched too thin, our focus collapses onto the next deadline, the next email, and the next interruption. Everything else falls away.

The cruel irony of tunnelling is that it creates a feedback loop, a vicious circle. The more we zero in on what is right in front of us, the more we neglect the systems, relationships, or decisions that would actually ease the scarcity. A professional buried in urgent emails has no space to design a process that would reduce the flood. A parent juggling schedules has no energy left to think about longer-term routines that would create calm. In chasing the immediate, we mortgage the future.

Scarcity also reshapes us as people. It makes us less rational because decisions are made in crisis mode rather than with perspective. It makes us less humane because empathy requires capacity. When we are consumed by our own tunnel, we have little bandwidth left to notice others, to read nuance, or to extend patience. And in the workplace, that blindness is costly. A manager under pressure may see only the missed deadline, not the hidden barriers a team is facing. Colleagues may stop recognising each other's efforts because they are too focused on their own survival. Entire teams can slip into tunnel vision, running ever faster on the treadmill of urgency while their long-term strategy gathers dust.

This is where capacity becomes more than a personal issue. It is also relational. You might be able to muscle through fatigue and distraction on your own, but when you arrive depleted, your colleagues feel it. Energy and mind are social currencies. People don't see your calendar, but they notice your presence. They can tell if you are attentive or distracted, calm or frantic, and engaged or resentful. Teams are constantly trading in this invisible currency, and the quality of those exchanges determines how much trust, creativity, and collaboration can flourish.

I saw this during a project with a mining leadership team. They were technically competent, committed, and hardworking. But they were also collectively exhausted. Urgency had become their only mode. Every meeting was a fire drill. In that climate, trust eroded. Colleagues began to guard information instead of sharing it, fearing that transparency would only add to their urgency. They became increasingly frustrated, easily triggered by one another. The turning point came when they deliberately worked on creating moments of space in between their chaotic workflow. A moment of pause and clarity between meetings. A moment of presence while making a cuppa. A few minutes at the end of the day to review. All of this shifted the tone—less rushed, less frantic, and more clarity. They also supported each other in this by actively working to not add to the noise. Energy changed, and with it, the whole capacity of the group.

Research backs this up. Barbara Fredrickson's broaden-and-build theory shows that positive emotions literally expand our field of vision. They make us more generous, more collaborative, and more creative. In contrast, negative emotions narrow our aperture. They make us tunnel, which means that enjoyment is not a form of indulgence. It is a design factor. Work that never includes enjoyment slowly strangles its own capacity.

Enjoyment also touches the personal core of why capacity matters. At some level, all of us want to end the day not just with a completed list but with a sense of meaning. We want to feel good about what we did and who we were while doing it. That sense of satisfaction—of being proud of the way you showed up, of having made a dent in something that matters—requires more than time management. It requires mental and emotional bandwidth. It requires capacity.

That sense of satisfaction—
of being proud of the
way you showed up, of
having made a dent in
something that matters—
requires more than time
management. It requires
mental and emotional
bandwidth. It requires
capacity.

Think about the difference between the days when you arrive home depleted, snappy, and unable to engage with the people you love, and the days when you arrive with something left to give. The work may not have looked very different. The number of hours may have been the same. The difference was capacity. This is why it matters so much. It matters for quality: your ability to think clearly, to solve problems, and to innovate. It matters for relationships: your ability to connect, to lead, and to respond rather than react. It matters for self-esteem: that quiet measure of whether your week added up to something you value. And it matters for sustainability. Burnout is not just an HR risk. It is a strategy risk. An organisation full of exhausted people cannot win.

For individuals, ignoring capacity is a form of self-neglect. We can survive for a while by running on adrenaline, by patching together bursts of focus. But over time, the cost is steep. Clarity declines, creativity wanes, health erodes, and relationships suffer. It is no coincidence that burnout is now one of the defining workplace challenges of our era. We designed for efficiency, not capacity. The irony is that designing for capacity does not mean doing less. It often means doing the same work with more presence, more energy, and more clarity. The output can, in fact, increase because the effort is channelled with focus instead of scattered with distraction. But even when output doesn't increase, the outcomes that matter most—the quality of decisions, the health of teams, and the sense of fulfilment—all grow stronger.

So, what does it look like to put capacity at the centre? In this book, I use a model that supports the core element of the mind—

how you can actively and purposefully work towards supporting your mind within your productivity. So that the invisible part, the section below the surface, stops running you off track without you being aware of it. It is the interaction of how you manage your workload, your communications, and your systems, in line with how your brain can function optimally. That you get to experience productivity as a complete ecosystem and have the ability to prioritise, to schedule, to focus, and to enjoy.

This is not a quick fix. It's a reframe. It's recognising that in a culture obsessed with busyness, it takes courage to pay attention to what is invisible. It takes courage to acknowledge that the hours in your day are not the same as the energy you can give to them, and that your mind is not a flawless container but a filter full of assumptions. It takes courage to design not just for doing, but for being.

In the chapters that follow, we will examine why we are overloaded, what the hard limits of our cognitive systems are, and how to design ways of working that protect and grow capacity rather than drain it. We will explore what it means to have the cognitive capacity to function effectively in a world of constant input.

However, before we proceed, let me leave you with this: if you have ever ended a week exhausted but dissatisfied, if you have ever wondered why doing more leaves you feeling less, if you have ever longed for work to feel meaningful again instead of mechanical—there is nothing wrong with you. You are not lazy or inefficient. You are human, living in a system that measures the visible and neglects the vital, invisible. Cognitive capacity matters because it is the foundation of everything else. It matters because without it, time management is an illusion, task lists are distractions, and even the best intentions collapse. It matters because with it, you can bring your best to the work that deserves it, and still have something left for the life that makes it worthwhile.

Ask Yourself:

- When did I last end a week feeling exhausted but oddly unsatisfied? What drained my capacity most?
- Where in my calendar do I confuse an open slot with genuine availability?
- What tasks in my week feel like treadmill motion rather than meaningful direction?
- When does my energy signal drop most consistently during the day? What triggers it?
- Which of the four elements of productivity—time, task, energy, and mind—do I tend to overemphasise, and which do I neglect?

CHAPTER 2

WHY WE ARE AT CAPACITY

You cannot overestimate the unimportance of practically everything.

—John Maxwell

It often begins before breakfast. You wake up, glance at your phone, and are greeted not by the promise of a fresh day but by the residue of the night: emails that arrived while you slept, notifications from messaging apps, updates from teams in different time zones, calendar reminders popping up, all before you've even had coffee. You scroll while brushing your teeth, mentally sorting through what deserves attention first, already behind on a day that hasn't started. By the time you open your laptop, you're juggling inputs from five different channels. A Teams chat ping interrupts an email you hadn't finished reading. Another calendar invite lands, slicing what was meant to be a focus block. Someone forwards a thread asking for "quick input," which is rarely quick. Even if the clock shows 9.45 in the morning, your brain feels like it's already noon.

And here's the thing: this feels normal. Everyone around you is operating at the same pace, reacting to the same flood. We shrug, laugh about being busy, and compare inbox numbers like war wounds. But normal doesn't mean healthy. The reality is that most professionals today are not just busy. They are overloaded. Not because they lack discipline or drive, but because they are trying to do their jobs in environments that never stop demanding more input, more response, more availability.

This chapter is not about offering fixes. It is about seeing the problem clearly enough that you stop blaming yourself. The system is wired for overload, and if you feel like you're barely keeping up, it's because you're human.

The Overload Epidemic

The press is the evil of the present age, and will corrupt the mind's noblest tendencies.

—SOREN KIERKEGAARD (1813–1855)

Researchers have a blunt way of describing what we're living through: an epidemic of overload. It's not a metaphor; it's measurable. Data reveals quantifiable increases in workload and communication demands across various sectors. This isn't subjective; it's a documented crisis. The measurable impact manifests in burnout, decreased productivity, and widespread mental health challenges. The documented increase in workload and communication isn't just anecdotal; hard data reveals a significant rise in demands across industries, leading to widespread burnout. This isn't simply a feeling; it's a measurable crisis affecting productivity and mental well-being. This overload manifests in various ways, from excessive meeting times and information-seeking struggles to the relentless barrage of emails and phone calls, creating a constant state of interruption and fragmented focus.

The impact on cognitive resources is substantial, exceeding the capacity of the human brain to handle. The resulting mental and emotional toll is undeniable, with a significant percentage of workers reporting feelings of exhaustion and depletion.

Research is ongoing to fully grasp the extent of this crisis. This emphasises the need for a systemic re-evaluation of work structures and expectations, paving the way for potential solutions and interventions.

A global study by Microsoft found that the number of meetings on its Teams platform more than doubled between early 2020 and 2022. Weekly meeting time surged by 252%. The average workday lengthened by forty-six minutes. Coordination time expanded, but focus time contracted. Most workers reported having fewer than two hours a day of uninterrupted time to think. Coveo's Workplace Relevance Report, surveying 4,000 employees, revealed that workers spend on average 3.6 hours each day just searching for information they need to do their jobs. That's nearly half the day lost to hunting. IT staff fared even worse, at 4.2 hours. And it isn't just wasted time; one in six employees said poor access to information made them want to quit.

The sheer volume of input is staggering. Employees receive, on average, 350 emails a week. For executives, the number spikes to up to 300 a day. That's the equivalent of reading 167 newspapers every day. Add in the phone pickups—surveys suggest an average of 400 times per day—and you get a picture of just how little uninterrupted time remains. Interruptions eat up nearly 28% of the workday. Each interruption doesn't just take seconds; research from Gloria Mark at the University of California, Irvine, shows it takes, on average, twenty-three minutes to return to the original task after a disruption. And the switching is relentless. The typical knowledge worker changes tasks every three minutes. No wonder people are frayed. Gallup's 2023 report found that 44% of workers feel emotionally depleted at the end of each day. The issue isn't just hours. It's cognitive load—the invisible tax of too many demands on a finite mind.

Here's a list of more alarming statistics in our epidemic of overload:

- Ringing phones and email alerts lower IQs by ten points.
- Knowledge workers spend an average of twenty hours a week managing email.
- Information overload costs the U.S. economy approximately $900 billion annually.
- 60% of computer users check email in the bathroom.
- 40% of early risers check emails by 6am to get ahead.
- A typical knowledge worker turns to email fifty to one hundred times a day.
- 85% of computer users say they would take a laptop on vacation.
- Employees consider one in three emails unnecessary.

- 26% of people want to delete all their email and start over.
- Employees visit an average of forty websites a day.
- Of the six emails that are ignored for a day, five are then ignored for good.
- Knowledge workers switch tasks every three minutes.
- 11% of people check email on the go.
- Email causes stress for 40% of knowledge workers.
- 46% of computer users say they are hooked on email.
- 85% of work emails are opened within two minutes.
- Interruptions eat up 28% of the workday.
- Email worsens the quality of life for 31% of workers.
- 60% of employees report experiencing high stress and burnout due to digital communication overload.
- Knowledge workers spend approximately 88% of their workweek on communication (messages, emails, chats), with around nineteen hours per week on written messaging alone.
- 55% of respondents feel that time is wasted trying to interpret or reply to messages.

Information Pollution

We are drowning in information, while starving for wisdom.

—**Biologist E.O. Wilson**

Think about how we usually talk about overload: as if it's simply "too much." Too many emails, too many meetings, and too many tools. That's true, but it's incomplete. The more insidious issue is that the information we are asked to process affects us, and I can best describe this phenomenon we're facing as information pollution.

Pollution is the right choice of word. With my background in environmental science, I chose this very intentionally. Like smog in a city, the particles are individually invisible, but collectively they harm us. Pollution accumulates over time, and although invisible, it poses a real danger. Just like we need to be warned about air pollution and take it very seriously, the same applies to information pollution. You may not notice the single irrelevant ping, but add them up across a day, and your mind is foggy, your patience thin, and your decisions rushed. It harms our performance, our quality of work, and our quality of life. It also isn't sustainable.

Herbert Simon warned in the 1970s:

A wealth of information creates a poverty of attention.

At the time, he was reflecting on how economic and social systems were beginning to shift toward information as the new scarce resource. But his words read as prophecy today. We've engineered tools, platforms, and workflows that maximise the sheer volume of information flowing into our lives, but do little to maximise its relevance. The paradox is striking: we have more data at our fingertips than any generation in history, yet clarity feels harder than ever to find. Studies show that 44% of the information retrieved in workplace searches is irrelevant. Employees must sift through noise before they can act. More than half of employees report needing to consult four or more systems just to locate a single piece of information—a task database here, a SharePoint site there, an email thread buried in Outlook, a Teams or Slack message lost in the scroll. Each additional step bleeds away focus and time.

And this isn't just about wasted minutes. Every irrelevant document scanned, every login screen navigated, every fruitless search eats into finite cognitive bandwidth. Instead of solving problems, taking action, or making decisions, employees burn capacity, searching for what they need in order to solve problems or make decisions. It is a silent tax on every knowledge worker, compounding across hours, days, and entire organisations.

In many workplaces, the irony is that the very systems designed to create transparency and access have ended up multiplying complexity. A finance team might store policies in one system, budgets in another, and conversations about both scattered across chat threads. A project team may have a dozen tools for scheduling, tracking, and reporting, none of which connect cleanly. The result is not empowerment but exhaustion—a sense of chasing shadows while the real work piles up. Simon's phrase—poverty of attention—is the most apt description of this condition. The scarcity is no longer in data. It is in the human ability to filter, interpret, and act with clarity. Until organisations acknowledge that attention is the most precious resource in the workplace, the overload epidemic will continue to erode both productivity and well-being.

Information is only one side of the equation. The other is complexity.

Modern work is less about routine and more about orchestration. Tasks are interdependent. Processes involve multiple systems. Projects span departments, time zones, and platforms. Instead of clear start and finish lines, many tasks feel like loops—never fully done, always demanding updates, check-ins, and reports.

A project engineer at a global firm once described his day: "Meetings, reports, interruptions, waiting on approvals. I do so much, but at the end, I'm not sure what I actually moved forward."

That sense of futility is common. You expend energy, but because the system is tangled, the progress is hard to see. Over time, the mismatch between effort and visible results erodes motivation. You feel inadequate, not because you lack skill, but because the environment is designed for inefficiency.

Studies of workplace complexity highlight common culprits: unclear goals, too many tools, overabundance of irrelevant information, constant task-switching, and pressure to report back on everything. Each adds friction. Together, they create a sense of drowning in detail. The outcomes are predictable: confusion, delayed decisions, loss of control, greater tolerance for error, stress, and anxiety. It's not that you're weak; it's that the structure itself multiplies strain.

If information pollution feels abstract, picture this: You're trying to drink from five fire hoses at once. Emails, Slack/Teams, dashboards, meetings, decisions—all blasting you simultaneously. It's not laziness that makes you falter. It's physics. The pressure is too high. Time-blocking a single hose doesn't solve it if the others are still hitting you in the face.

One director I coached broke down mid-call—not from exhaustion in the hours sense but from sheer decision fatigue. By 11am, she had already made a dizzying number of micro-decisions: which email to answer first, whether to accept a meeting, how to interpret a message, whether to forward something, and whether to say yes. None were large. But the accumulation shredded her clarity.

You feel inadequate, not
because you lack skill, but
because the environment
is designed for inefficiency.

Roy Baumeister's research on decision fatigue shows that willpower is finite. The more choices we face, the poorer our decisions become. Eventually, we default to avoidance, impulsivity, or collapse. This leader didn't need a vacation. She needed guardrails—off-switches for micro-decisions. Once she created criteria for what deserved her attention, her clarity returned almost instantly. That's the paradox of overload caused by information pollution. It's not usually the giant decisions that undo us. It's the drip, drip, drip of constant micro-choices under fire-hose pressure.

Overload, Overwhelm, Overwork

Information pollution doesn't just slow us down; it muddies perception, drains energy, and frays resilience. This is where language matters. Many of the high-performing professionals I work with come to me with the same complaint: "I'm exhausted, I'm confused, I'm drained—but I don't know why." The word they reach for most often is "busy." But busy is too blunt. It hides the fact that there are actually different shades of strain, and knowing which one you're experiencing is half the battle.

Overload is too much input. Emails, pings, decisions, requests—all at once, all competing for attention. Your brain is bombarded and can't filter what matters. The result? Focus collapses. You can't think straight.

Overwhelm is the emotional reaction to that flood. It shows up as anxiety, avoidance, irritability, or even tears. You lose your spark, not because you lack discipline, but because your nervous system is overloaded. It feels like everything is urgent, and you don't know where to start.

Overwork is the grind of too much output. You keep delivering, helping, fixing, saying yes. Day after day, the weight accumulates. Your body and energy give way, and eventually the quality of your work suffers.

Think of it like carrying a backpack. Overload is someone dropping ten heavy books into the bag at once. Overwhelm is not knowing which to pull out first. Overwork is carrying the bag every day without a break. Your shoulders ache in all cases, but the strategy differs—drop weight, organise, or pause. Each state feels different—and each requires a different strategy. Overload needs filters. Overwhelm needs relief and recovery. Overwork needs rest. Treating them all as "busy" is like handing the same medicine to three different patients. In most workplaces, though, all three conditions are collapsed into that one word: busy. And busy is a terrible diagnosis. It obscures what's really happening and leads us to reach for the wrong fixes. Until we learn to distinguish overload from overwhelm and overwork, we'll keep mismanaging our energy, mistaking symptoms for causes. By naming the different ways this pressure shows up—input, emotion, and output—we can stop treating them as one blurred experience and start responding with more precision. It helps to separate three words often used interchangeably.

On a recent trip to Tokyo, I experienced overload and overwhelm, and the difference between them firsthand. New city, new client, new culture, new language. Everything was stimulating and exciting, but also a bit much. This was definitely overload. On the last day, though, leaving my hotel at 5.15am, the travel to the airport was less than ideal. First of all, the access to the correct train line was under construction, and navigating with a suitcase and all through the humongous train station was a challenge. Then, an accident on the train line put me in a scramble—I was on my way to the airport and had to decide whether to get off the train or stay on, hoping the time buffer I had that morning would be sufficient. I got off, booked myself an Uber (which, at this point, I was not the only one). I got onto another train line, had to adjust my train ticket, and then stressed about getting into Tokyo Haneda airport. After checking in, I rushed to customs to see the longest line of people I have ever experienced. It took me fifty minutes in that line. What I had hoped would be a joyful final exploration of Tokyo suddenly tipped into stress.

I realised I was overwhelmed. It was purely emotional. It all felt too much—much like when I arrived and found my feet a few days earlier—but this time it was pure stress around elements I had no control over and felt very challenging to navigate through. It's that awareness that matters. By noticing that I was overwhelmed, I recognised that I had an emotional reaction, and then I managed it. I was able to rationalise, have plan B in place, and take action on what I had control over, while also giving space to my emotions and being okay that I wasn't okay. Too often at work, we miss that step of identifying what is really going on. We push through, and perhaps a different strategy is all that we need.

The Messy Middle

When you tidy your space, you tidy your mind.

—**Marie Kondo**

Despite these plethora of challenges we face with information, information is of tremendous value to us. But we don't process information just to know. We process it to change. To act. To move forward. But most of us aren't in control of the messy middle—the stage where raw data becomes filtered, sorted, and integrated into meaning.

Think of your mind like a unicellular organism, like an amoeba. Floating in its environment, it has a wonderful protective layer—the cell membrane. Its membrane decides what gets in and what doesn't. Without a membrane, everything floods in, and the organism dies. With a strong membrane, it can filter, absorb nutrients, and thrive. This organism is very intentional with what it lets in and what it fights off.

Our cognitive membrane should be seen as that same protective layer. Without it, everything enters—noise, stress, irrelevance. With it, we can absorb what's valuable and block what isn't. The issue today is not just that input has grown but that our membranes are weak. Work cultures reward openness, availability, and responsiveness. Few reward discernment, let alone elimination. Due to the amount of data we face, we are losing our ability to process it effectively.

Research on situational awareness gives us a helpful lens to see why overload feels so corrosive. Mica Endsley, one of the leading scholars in the field, describes situational awareness as having three levels: perception (noticing inputs), comprehension (making sense of them), and projection (using them to anticipate what comes next). Most breakdowns don't occur because we fail to see the signals; they occur because we fail to interpret them.

Think of an air traffic controller: the radar screen lights up with aircraft. Perception is not the problem—they can see the blips. The challenge is comprehension: What does each blip mean in relation to the others? Which are potential conflicts? Which are safe? Without comprehension, the picture is fragmented dots, not a meaningful map. That same pattern plays out in offices every day. Emails arrive, chat messages ping, reports are shared, and dashboards update. Perception is easy: we "see" the inputs. But comprehension falters. We can't connect them into a coherent picture. We miss how one update changes the risk profile of a project, or how a small request signals a bigger shift in priorities. When comprehension fails, projection— the ability to plan effectively—never gets off the ground.

The human brain is, at its core, a prediction machine. It builds models of the world to reduce uncertainty, filter input, and respond efficiently. This works beautifully when the environment is structured, patterned, and coherent. But when the external world becomes chaotic—cluttered inboxes, inconsistent signals, conflicting priorities—the brain's internal model clashes with what it perceives outside. The result is stress, confusion, and fatigue.

I once worked for a CFO who embodied this clash. His desk was a mountain of paper, sticky notes, and reports. "Organised chaos," he called it. But his team saw the reality: missed follow-ups, double work, and delayed approvals. Contrast that with a different office I visited where physical spaces mirrored mental clarity: a brainstorming room with floor-to-ceiling whiteboards, a reading nook for reflection, and open areas designed for social interaction. The environment itself cued purpose.

Environmental psychology confirms what we intuitively know. Clutter elevates cortisol, the body's stress hormone. Studies of "forest bathing" in Japan show that structured, organic environments—trees, streams, predictable natural rhythms—lower heart rate, improve mood, and restore cognitive clarity. Nature calms because it offers complexity with coherence. Offices often offer complexity without coherence. When the environment is noisy, our ability to judge what's useful collapses. Like animals searching for food in a cluttered landscape, we dart from one patch to another, grabbing scraps, but never staying long enough to gather what we truly need.

Layer onto this the brutal limits of working memory. For decades, George Miller's famous "7±2" rule set the benchmark: we can hold only a handful of chunks of information at once. More recent research suggests it may be closer to four. Once you exceed that capacity, the system doesn't just slow down—it fails. Ideas drop off the edge. The conversation you had an hour ago evaporates. The brilliant thought you meant to write down is gone. You are literally at capacity.

The cost is not only exhaustion, it is that we lose meaning. You may process hundreds of inputs in a day—messages read, meetings attended, notifications acknowledged. But if none of those fragments integrate into a coherent thread, you end the day with a hollow feeling, as if nothing actually happened. The brain has been busy, but not productive. Activity has replaced progress.

This is the hidden danger of overload: not just that we work harder, but that we lose the storyline. Without comprehension, work dissolves into noise. And without projection, we lose our ability to steer. What's left is a sense of futility—the feeling of running all day without moving forward.

Our mind is designed to make sense of the world. Overload it and it will reach capacity. Rather than try to deal with the external surplus of input, we need to make it our job to help our mind to do its job better. We need to create a strong membrane that functions as a cognitive boundary. So it can let in what's valuable (insight, relevance, connection) and blocks what's not (noise, repetition, excess). Without it, we don't just get tired—we lose the ability to make sense of our world. You don't need more storage—you need smarter filters.

The Myth of More

There is more to life than increasing its speed.

—MAHATMA GANDHI

Now we know our worlds are full—full of information, options, etc., do you realise that our entire environment is designed to hijack our attention? The brain evolved to scan for new stimuli—a survival instinct. Today, the same wiring is triggered by endless notifications, posts, and updates.

We mistake novelty for knowledge. A podcast here, an article there, a scroll between meetings. But consuming without consolidating is like eating all day without digesting. The body becomes bloated, tired, and sluggish. The mind does too.

Our mind is designed to make sense of the world. Overload it and it will reach capacity. Rather than try to deal with the external surplus of input, we need to make it our job to help our mind to do its job better.

A strategy lead I worked with listened to three podcasts a day, skimmed newsletters at lunch, and kept thirty tabs open "just in case." When it came time to make a strategic call, he froze. "I've read everything," he admitted. "But I still don't know what I think." The shift came when he set one rule: no new input after 3pm, only consolidation. Within a week, his insights deepened. He wasn't learning before; he was hoarding.

The myth of more says that if we consume more information, say yes to more requests, and work more hours, we'll get better results. But more often, the opposite is true. We end up shallow, scattered, and depleted. Neuroscience explains why. Dopamine rewards novelty. Each ping, each scroll, each refresh delivers a micro-hit. But dopamine drives wanting, not satisfaction. You crave more but feel no fuller.

This craving is not accidental. Tristan Harris, a former Google ethicist, has shown how platforms exploit this craving for unpredictability. They are engineered to hook, not to help. Infinite scroll, autoplay, push alerts, and algorithmically timed notifications are built on the same principles as slot machines: unpredictability fuels compulsion. The less predictable the reward—when will the next "like" arrive, the next email land, the next message buzz?—the more powerfully the loop entrenches itself. Netflix CEO, Reed Hastings, famously said, "You get a show or a movie you're really dying to watch, and you end up staying up late at night, so we actually compete with sleep. ... And we're winning!"

We are not just dealing with more data. We are managing more decisions, more demands, more pressure to respond. Input floods exceed filters. Decisions pile up faster than we can process.

Emotional reserves drain. Environments clash with our brain's need for order and sense-making. Our culture glorifies busyness. Tools accelerate volume without wisdom. It is no wonder professionals feel constantly behind. The problem is not laziness or disorganisation. It is structural, systemic, and global. And the costs are enormous: to our productivity, our health, our relationships, and our sense of meaning.

Let's pause here. Before we rush to solutions in later chapters, we need to sit with the weight of this. If you feel scattered, impatient, or perpetually behind, it's not because you're failing. It *is* because you're failing, isn't it? That's what the inner voice screams. It's because you're operating in an environment designed for overload. You are not weak; you are human. And humans have limits. Overload is not a personal flaw. It is the predictable outcome of systems that value speed over sense, volume over clarity, and availability over focus. You are operating in a world that makes failing inevitable. The challenge—and the hope—is that once we see this clearly, we can begin to design differently.

Ask Yourself:

- Where in my week do I feel the fire hoses blasting—too many inputs at once—and what does that do to my clarity?

- When have I noticed "information pollution"—irrelevant emails, pings, or dashboards—and how does that clutter affect my focus?

- What have I learned from understanding the difference between overloaded, overwhelmed, and overworked?

- If I could drop one "book" from my metaphorical backpack this week—an input, an obligation, or an output—what difference would it make?

CHAPTER 3

WHAT LIMITS YOUR COGNITIVE CAPACITY

Never before in history has the human brain been asked to track so many moving parts.

—BRENÉ BROWN

Think about what your brain is being asked to do on an average day. You wake up to a phone full of notifications, emails, and messages. You're expected to know the status of multiple projects, recall details from conversations days ago, make a dozen decisions before lunch, and keep your emotions steady while the environment around you constantly changes. Brené Brown's observation is painfully true: we are running mental marathons in conditions no generation before us ever had to endure.

Chapter 2 was about seeing the scale of overload in our world; this chapter continues about understanding the limits of our minds within our environment. Because while technology has given us infinite access to information, our cognitive systems remain stubbornly finite. We are not designed to process thousands of inputs, juggle competing priorities, and make continuous micro-decisions without consequence. The result isn't just fatigue—it's reduced performance, fractured focus, and the sense of falling behind even when we're working harder than ever.

To make sense of why, we need to talk about the saboteurs of cognitive capacity. These are the hidden and obvious forces that hijack our bandwidth. Some are internal—patterns of thought and behaviour that live inside us. Others are external—loud, visible pressures from the environment. Together, they pull our mental strings until we feel like performers in a circus we never auditioned for.

It's Like a Circus

Imagine your brain is running a full circus, but you're the only one on stage. You're trying to juggle, walk a tightrope, and manage the show all at once. The spotlight is hot, the audience is loud, and acts keep being added without rehearsal. That's what it feels like to live with cognitive saboteurs: too many roles, too much noise, and not enough capacity to hold it all.

Let's start with the performers inside the tent—the internal saboteurs.

Unintentionality—The Drifting Clown

In every circus, there's a clown, stumbling from act to act, reacting to whatever happens. In our mental circus, this is unintentionality: drifting through the day without clear choices, letting everything else decide for us. When you don't set intention, you spend your energy reacting. The inbox dictates what you do next. The phone buzz decides where your attention goes. You end the day exhausted but unclear on what you actually achieved. Without intention, there is no filter. And without a filter, there is no focus. This saboteur is subtle because it often masquerades as productivity. You're busy, answering messages, jumping into tasks, and helping colleagues. But busyness without direction is a cognitive drain. Like the clown, you may look active, but underneath, you're scattered.

Ambiguity—The Confused Ringmaster

Next in the circus is the ringmaster—the one who's meant to orchestrate the acts. But in our version, the ringmaster has lost the program. Instructions are vague, goals are fuzzy, and cues are unclear. This is the saboteur of ambiguity. When you're given a task without clarity—a vague email, a half-specified request, an unclear decision—your brain burns energy not on the doing, but on the figuring out. What does this mean? What's expected? What's the outcome? The mental effort that could have gone into progress is consumed by interpretation. Research shows that uncertainty itself is stressful. When the brain can't predict what's required, it stays on high alert, scanning for cues. That's why unclear instructions drain so much more energy than specific ones. It's not the size of the task; it's the fog around it.

Indecision—The Tightrope Walker

Picture yourself on a tightrope, stepping forward and back, unable to commit. That's what indecision feels like. Every unmade decision hangs in your mind like an open tab, consuming space and energy. We like to tell ourselves that not deciding keeps options open. But in reality, a decision not made is still a decision—one that squats on your bandwidth. Loops of "what if" and "should I" run in the background, like a program consuming RAM. This saboteur is especially cruel to perfectionists. Fear of making the wrong choice leads to no choice at all, which compounds pressure. The longer a decision sits undecided, the more weight it carries. The tightrope feels higher, the fall more dangerous, the paralysis stronger. And yet, once a decision is made, energy is released. The act of choosing clears the mental loop. It's not the choice itself that drains us, but the suspension of it.

Remembering—The Overloaded Juggler

Now imagine a juggler, tossing balls higher and higher, trying to keep them all in the air. That's your brain when you use it as a storage unit. "Don't forget to call back. Remember that deadline. Keep track of those client's details." Working memory is finite. When you fill it with reminders, you leave less space for problem-solving, creativity, and planning. The brain isn't designed to store dozens of "don't forgets" while also solving complex problems. The symptoms of this saboteur are familiar: restless sleep, forgetfulness, irritability. You wake up at 3am remembering something you meant to do. You feel guilty for dropping balls. The juggling act doesn't end when you leave the office. Productivity experts like David Allen have long argued for externalising memory—writing things down, creating trusted systems. Because the more your brain juggles, the less it creates.

Expectations & Assumptions—The Trickster

Finally, meet the trickster: expectations and assumptions. You may expect a task to be easy, or you overcomplicate it in your head. You may assume someone understands what you meant. You may have high expectations of yourself, or you feel pressure that others put those expectations on you. In any of these scenarios, you are not being realistic—you either underestimate or overestimate, but the result is that you trick yourself. When reality doesn't match, frustration follows. The energy drain is not from the task itself but from managing disappointment, rework, and confusion. This takes up much more of your cognitive capacity. Bias also plays a role here. Expectations and assumptions shape what we notice, what we ignore, and how we interpret events. They are filters—and when faulty, they warp the entire show.

These five internal saboteurs—unintentionality, ambiguity, indecision, remembering, and expectations & assumptions—are like circus acts running amok inside your own head. They're not malicious; they're human. But they consume capacity, pulling energy away from the work that matters.

If the internal saboteurs are the circus performers on stage, the external saboteurs are the unruly audience and chaotic environment around them. Even if you could master the internal noise, you still have to contend with the shouting, interruptions, and shifting demands from the outside world.

Noise—The Heckling Crowd

Every circus has background noise: the chatter of the crowd, the rustle of programs, the distractions at the edges. In our mental circus, this is noise: irrelevant information, visual clutter, overflowing inboxes, endless threads. Even if you "ignore" them, your brain doesn't. Filtering noise still takes energy. That's why open-plan offices feel so draining—your brain is working overtime to suppress irrelevant sights and sounds. It's why an inbox full of unread emails still feels heavy. Noise adds friction, even when you're not consciously attending to it.

Distractions—The Pokes and Interruptions

Now imagine trying to balance on a tightrope while being poked every few minutes. That's the effect of distractions. Notifications, alerts, colleagues interrupting, context switching. Gloria Mark's research at UC Irvine shows that after an interruption, it takes an average of twenty-three minutes to return to the original task. Multiply that across a day, and you see why focus feels elusive. You're not just losing minutes—you're dragging the residue of each switch into the next task. Distractions fragment attention. They keep you shallow when your work requires depth. The performer is constantly starting over, never building momentum.

High Quantity, Low Quality—Fifty Acts in Fifteen Minutes

Picture being handed a program with fifty acts to perform in just fifteen minutes. None rehearsed, most of them irrelevant. That's the saboteur of high quantity and low quality. Every day we face an avalanche of inputs: emails, reports, articles, posts, documents. But much of it is low value. You skim everything, retain nothing, and feel perpetually behind. This feeds "just in case" hoarding and FOMO (fear of missing out). You keep tabs open, files saved, newsletters unread—just in case you might need them. But the pile grows, the signal weakens, and your brain carries the weight of all that deferred processing. The result is mental indigestion: stuffed with information, starved of meaning.

Inconsistency—The Changing Program

Imagine if the circus program changed halfway through the show. Acts shuffled, instructions contradicted, tools swapped out. That's inconsistency. In work, inconsistency shows up as shifting priorities, unclear communication, double-handling, and rework. Systems that aren't stable enough for your brain to build habits. Instead of trusting the process, you burn energy re-learning and re-checking. Inconsistency breeds distrust. You don't know if the tool will work, if the request will stand, or if the goal will hold. And so your brain stays on guard, which comes at a high cost.

Complexity—The Over-Engineered Act

Finally, there's complexity—the over-engineered trapeze routine with far too many steps. Complexity looks impressive, but kills clarity. Overly detailed processes, bloated documents, and workflows that require unnecessary approvals. The brain thrives on simplicity and repeatable patterns. Complexity demands extra cognitive load just to understand what's happening before you can act. We often confuse complexity with importance. But in practice, complexity is a capacity killer. It slows decision-making, invites errors, and drains energy.

Put the saboteurs together and you see why capacity feels scarce. Inside the tent, you're juggling, tightrope walking, clowning, and cleaning up all at once. Outside, the crowd is noisy, the program keeps changing, the demands pile up, and the acts grow more complicated. These ten saboteurs, five internal and five external, hijack your capacity. Paying attention to them and realising which ones are at play are essential for designing a more effective workflow.

Modes of Work

Now that we've identified the ten saboteurs of your cognitive capacity, let's look at how they play out in practice. How you handle these directly impacts your capacity. The output and quality of your work and how exhausted (or not) you are at the end of the day are a result of your management of these saboteurs. The model below shows you which level you operate in, what your focus should be, and your productivity rating. The model maps the work modes people slip into depending on how well—or poorly—their capacity is protected. When I work with people, this is how we assess how well they are doing in managing their cognitive capacity.

CAPACITY	ANTICIPATE	4X
SUSTAINABLE	MENTAL LOAD MANAGEMENT	3X
HARD	INFORMATION PROCESSING	2X
BUSY	DECISION MAKING	1X
FRANTIC	METHODS & SYSTEMS	-1X
CRISIS	RECTIFICATION	-2X

Crisis Work Mode

At the lowest mode, you're in constant firefighting. Every ping feels urgent, every problem lands at your feet, and you spend the day reacting. Lots of avoidable mistakes happen that you need to correct. Deadlines and even simple requests get missed or ignored. You may work long hours, but with little to show beyond exhaustion. This is survival mode: highly ineffective and deflating.

The focus needs to be on the immediate rectification of your workflow. Establish core priorities, gather resources to get the job done, and work from one source that dictates what needs action. Everything else does not require your attention.

Frantic Work Mode

Slightly better, but still draining. Here, you're running—meetings, messages, tasks—without space to breathe. You're producing, but the quality suffers, and you rarely feel on top of things. Your productivity is still unimpactful. Frantic mode is exhausting, and you work without intention and reactively. Like spinning plates, you're terrified of letting one fall. It's chaos. We are the cliché of the rat in the wheel; we are stressed and exhausted. You feel you let yourself and others down. We seem to be doing it all, yet our output is not sufficient.

The focus should be on setting up methods and systems that support you, that help you not to rely on memory, and that are consistent and trustworthy.

Busy Work Mode

This is the most socially accepted mode. You're checking things off, answering emails, sitting in meetings, and feeling "productive." But much of it is low value. Busy mode is comfortable because it looks like you're working hard—and you are—but the impact is shallow. It's a plateau where many professionals live without realising it. You have good days and bad days, but you need a holiday to look forward to if you want to stay engaged. You feel driven by urgency, and work is draining.

The focus needs to be on your decision-making; the quality of your decisions will dictate the quality of your day. Rather than letting activity rule your day, you need to make it meaningful.

Hard Work Mode

This one is deceiving because the output is noticeable, but it requires hard work. You're pushing through with determination and sheer effort. Output is happening, but at the cost of energy. You put in extra hours to get the job done, but your list never seems to be finished. You feel you're thriving and making an impact, but complaints from your loved ones show that this is not sustainable. Productivity doubles compared to being stuck in busyness, but it doesn't feel easy or light. You're using willpower to keep going, and fatigue builds. Hard work mode gets things done, but cracks are starting to show.

The focus needs to be on effective information processing. How do you handle input, filter it effectively, and avoid cognitive overload? By deliberately structuring how you take in, sort, and act on information, you can move into a much more manageable and smarter workflow.

Sustainable Work Mode

In this mode, saboteurs are recognised and managed. You have clearer filters, stronger boundaries, and more focus. You're managing your mental load, balancing effort with recovery, and starting to experience consistency. Work is no longer reactive or forceful—it feels manageable and considered. Sustainable mode multiplies your productivity because you're not burning out with every step. Instead, you're pacing yourself and using systems that support clarity. Stress levels lower, energy steadies, and quality improves. This is where resilience starts to build.

The focus needs to be on mental load management. This means externalising what you carry, preventing clutter in your mind, and structuring work so it flows rather than clogs. Sustainable mode is about managing your capacity so it doesn't leak away.

Capacity Work Mode

In this mode, you are clear, calm, and intentional. Here, you're not just doing work, you're sustaining energy, creativity, and resilience. You can zoom out, think strategically, and align your actions with purpose. In capacity mode, you're equipped to handle challenges without depleting yourself. You leave room for recovery and reflection, which means performance is both higher and more sustainable. Here, productivity is amplified—not by doing more, but by focusing on what counts. This is not about intensity but about alignment: doing the right things at the right time, with clarity. It feels both impactful and sustainable, and it is deeply satisfying.

The focus needs to be on anticipation. This is about knowing that your work path isn't a straight line and being prepared for, rather than surprised by, new input. When you operate in capacity mode, you are at your most effective—4X your output compared to the lower modes—because your mental bandwidth is fully intact.

The purpose of the value model isn't to label you as "bad" or "good." It's to give you a mirror. By noticing whether you're operating in crisis, frantic, busy, hard, sustainable, or capacity mode, you gain awareness of the patterns that dictate your days. That awareness is powerful. If you know you're stuck in frantic mode, you can ask why. If you recognise you're plateauing in busy mode, you can choose to shift. Without this understanding, it's easy to assume your stress is just the way work has to be. With it, you realise you have more ownership than you think. The key question isn't, "Am I always in capacity?"—nobody is. The key is, "Which mode do I spend most of my time in, and is that serving me?" When you start paying attention to your mode, you create the possibility of change. You can't control every saboteur, but you can design your environment and your responses to spend more time in sustainable and capacity mode, and less in crisis and frantic mode.

Most workplaces hover between frantic and busy mode. Sustainable mode is rare. Operating at full capacity is rarer still. But naming the modes helps us see the cost of the circus—and the possibility of a calmer stage.

Never before in history has the human brain been asked to track so many moving parts. We are running a circus with no crew, no intermissions, and a crowd that never stops yelling. Understanding the saboteurs matters because it reframes the problem. You're not failing because you're weak. You're struggling because you are human—a human with finite bandwidth, finite memory, finite energy. The path forward is not harder hustle, but wiser design: learning to cancel acts, quiet the noise, and align environments with the brain's natural strengths.

Ask Yourself:

- Which internal saboteur do I wrestle with most: unintentionality, ambiguity, indecision, remembering, or assumptions?
- Which external saboteur feels loudest in my environment: noise, distractions, low-quality inputs, inconsistency, or complexity?
- What's one "act" in my circus I could cancel, simplify, or shield this week that could protect my capacity?
- Looking at the six levels in the work mode model, which mode am I operating in most often: crisis, frantic, busy, hard, sustainable, or capacity?
- What is most important to me: my output or my mental well-being?

CHAPTER 4

HOW TO CREATE COGNITIVE CAPACITY

It's not information overload. It's filter failure.

—Clay Shirky

You walk into the supermarket for one thing: milk. Ten minutes later, you're standing in the cereal aisle, staring at forty-seven different boxes. Cornflakes, bran flakes, oats, oats with chia, oats with berries, sugar-free granola, paleo granola, gluten-free muesli, five brands of each, each with competing promises. Somewhere along the way, you've forgotten about the milk. It's a small moment, but it illustrates something bigger. Our environments are designed for abundance. Choice is everywhere, input is everywhere, noise is everywhere. The modern world isn't built around limits—it's built on excess. And our brains, ancient as they are, are caught in the middle.

Clay Shirky has the cleanest explanation for this: It's not information overload; it's filter failure. The volume is real, but volume isn't the villain. What drains your capacity is that too much gets in, too little is sorted, and almost nothing is cleanly closed. We don't have our filter set up, and that means everything passes through.

A century ago, filters were baked into the environment. Editors curated news. Letters took days, and making trivial requests was too expensive to send. Work arrived through a single physical inbox; triage was visible and slow by design. Today, the gates are gone. Every tool can reach you instantly, cheaply, and repeatedly. The world switched from scarcity to abundance, but our filtering didn't keep pace. If filters don't protect that resource, noise wins by default. The result is exactly what Shirky warned us about: not that we have too much information, but that we fail to protect our minds from the excess.

Another way to go into the supermarket is to know what you need beforehand. You check your pantry, do your meal planning, and know you need milk, and you know your family's favourite cereal. That means when you enter the supermarket, your journey will go much smoother. The interaction will be simpler. It will take less energy, it will take less time, and it will be less frustrating. It will take less of your cognitive capacity.

Think back about that unicellular organism that's happily floating in its environment and thriving. That membrane serves a really crucial function—to not let everything in. So we need to start learning and applying that to ourselves in our daily lives. Create those filters so we remove noise and are left with what is valuable, useful, and timely.

Think about the different places where filters are supposed to live:

- **Personal filters**. Your criteria for what deserves attention, your capacity to ignore, the boundaries you set around time and availability. When these are vague, every input gets equal rights to your mind. You default to what is loudest or latest, not what is most important.

- **Tool filters.** Notification settings, inbox rules, channel etiquette, calendar norms, do-not-disturb windows. When these are left at their factory defaults, you inherit someone else's attention model—usually "interrupt me for everything."

- **Team and organisational filters**. Do we write agendas? Who needs to be CC'd? What does "urgent" mean? Where does a draft live, and when is it final? When the culture doesn't decide, chaos decides. Everyone builds their own micro-system, and the whole becomes fragmented and brittle.

When filters fail at any of these layers, your day shifts into constant triage. You touch everything briefly and move almost nothing meaningfully. There are four common modes of filter failure you'll recognise instantly. Once you see these failure modes, everyday pain points snap into focus.

- **Too porous.** Everything gets in. Every notification is on. Every request is accepted. You're copied on threads you don't need and added to meetings "just in case." Your attention is the open-plan office of your mind: no doors, no walls, everyone can walk through.

- **Too sticky**. Nothing gets out. Tasks start but don't end. Files are half-drafted. Decisions linger. Unfinished work keeps whispering, "Don't forget me." You go home full of fragments.
- **Too slow.** The world moves faster than your sorting does. By the time you've worked out what matters, three more inputs have landed. You never quite catch up, and that lag becomes low-grade anxiety.
- **Too hidden.** Filters exist, but they're invisible. You have criteria in your head that no one else knows. Your team has unwritten rules about who approves what. Tools have buried settings you never changed. Hidden filters create mismatched expectations and rework.

Overwhelmed by constant interruptions, productivity plummets. Prioritisation becomes impossible. Delayed responses and unfinished projects accumulate, creating stress. Hidden rules cause confusion and wasted effort. Identifying these filter failures allows for proactive solutions and improved workflow. A clearer path to efficiency emerges.

Sofia, a production manager, starts Monday determined to "focus." At 8.42am, she opens Teams "just to check" and spots three @mentions. One is genuine; two could wait. All three pull her in. Meanwhile, a document she's been "meaning to finish" sits open in a tab, nagging. By 10.15am, she had touched ten things but finished none. It's tempting to call this a willpower problem. It isn't. Sofia's filters are failing in three places: what gets in (no clear criteria for where to start), how work is grouped (everything is mixed together, so switching costs pile up), and how things end (nothing gets a clean

Identifying these filter failures allows for proactive solutions and improved workflow. A clearer path to efficiency emerges.

"done," so the mind can't release it). Her day isn't hard because she lacks grit; it's hard because her filtration is misconfigured.

Think of the Netflix paralysis you probably have felt at night. The platform offers thousands of choices, and the only thing your brain wants after a tiring and trying day is relief. Without a filter ("tonight I want one 30-minute light comedy"), your thumb keeps scrolling. Barry Schwartz calls this the paradox of choice: more options promise freedom but deliver indecision and regret. The problem isn't the library. It's that we arrived without a filter.

Here's a corporate version. A well-meaning team leader creates a culture of "inclusion" by CC'ing five extra leaders on every decision thread. The intention is good; the result is an explosion of replies, most of which do not add value. Or worse yet, some go off topic, and a new discussion starts in the same thread. Accountability blurs. People feel duty-bound to weigh in on work they don't own. What you're witnessing is a team-level filter failure—nothing is clear.

Decision fatigue ramps all of this. Roy Baumeister's research demonstrated that self-control and decision-making draw from the same finite pool of mental energy. Each choice, no matter how small, spends a little of that reserve. It doesn't matter whether you're choosing what tie to wear, which email to answer first, or who to hire—the act of choosing drains willpower. Over the course of a day, the pool runs low. And when it does, judgment falters. In his famous studies, Baumeister and colleagues used experiments with food choices and self-control tasks to show how people's ability to resist temptation or persist on difficult problems weakened after making a series of decisions. The phenomenon became known as ego depletion: the idea that willpower, like a muscle, tires with use.

Later research found similar effects in legal settings: judges were more likely to deny parole just before lunch or at the end of long stretches on the bench, not because cases were weaker, but because their cognitive reserves were depleted.

When filters are weak, you burn power on low-stakes choices all day—what to open, where to click, whether to respond—leaving less for the decisions that actually move the work. This is why some top executives standardise small things (same breakfast, fixed morning routine, templated agendas, same outfits). They're not being fussy; they're protecting the filter so that the day's limited decision budget goes to what matters.

There's also the problem of defaults. Most tools work the same way: notifications on, badges red, sounds enabled, inboxes mixing promotions with people, channels set to @all. If you never change defaults, you're choosing a porous way of working. The platforms are not evil; they're indifferent. They are designed to maximise engagement; it's your duty to maximise clarity. Changing defaults is a practical expression of filter strength.

And then there's culture. Words like "ASAP," "quick question," "just five minutes," and "for visibility" are cultural solvents that dissolve filters. Over time, they make responsiveness feel virtuous and boundaries feel rude. Healthy teams invert that norm. They make context the default (why you've been included, what decision is needed, by when), they separate FYIs from decisions, and they normalise saying no to things that don't meet criteria. That's not cold; that's considerate.

Two final truths about filters make them feel less like restriction and more like liberation. A lot of people I start working with initially find it extremely difficult to put this filter in place. When we are used to letting it all in and have, in a way, found our own—albeit perhaps failing—process of managing it all, it's hard to let go and put those boundaries in place.

First, a good filter reduces guilt. Much of modern professional guilt is phantom guilt: a sense you're letting people down because you can't say yes to everything. Clear filters convert guilt into choices. "This doesn't meet our criteria right now" or "I don't have capacity for that right now" is kinder and more honest than a half-hearted yes that creates hidden work and resentment.

Second, a good filter increases meaning. Meaning isn't found by adding more; it emerges when what you take in connects to what you care about and is carried through to completion. I recall a Sunday afternoon when I had a moment to myself. At that time, I was still working in my environmental management job, and my husband and I, besides both working full-time, also started our martial arts school. So on this Sunday afternoon, after finishing all the household tasks, the social obligations, and the administration for the martial arts school, I finally sat down and had time for myself. I had about an hour or two for some quality time for myself. Besides a cup of tea, next to my favourite chair, I had with me my iPad with an episode I wanted to watch, my digital SLR camera with a few tutorials I still needed to go through, two books I was currently reading, my red nail polish to do my toe nails for the week, and a Dutch magazine a friend gave to me to read. How on earth did I think I could do all those things within the next one to two hours before it would be dinner prep time?

Instead of looking forward to a couple of hours of unwinding me-time, I put pressure on myself by wanting to do too much and feeling totally overwhelmed. But these were my favourite hobbies, and I either wanted to do too much or didn't have enough time.

It made me realise "we do this to ourselves"! Now that the world gives us too much, it is imperative that we create the right filter to handle it.

Up to now, we've explored why capacity matters, how overload is suffocating us, and what limits exist within the human brain. Time to shift gears. Here, we look at the scaffolding of the solution—a way to think about cognitive capacity not as an endless fight against abundance, but as a system that works with our limitations instead of against them.

Let me introduce you to the Filter Framework. At the core, we have three elements: Criteria, Chunking, and Closure. Together, they form the framework for creating cognitive capacity. At their intersections sit three qualities—Meaningful, Methodical, and Manageable—which deepen the model and guide how we can make work and life feel lighter, clearer, and more productive.

We'll explore each one in detail later. For now, this chapter is about sketching the outline: giving you a map of how capacity can be built.

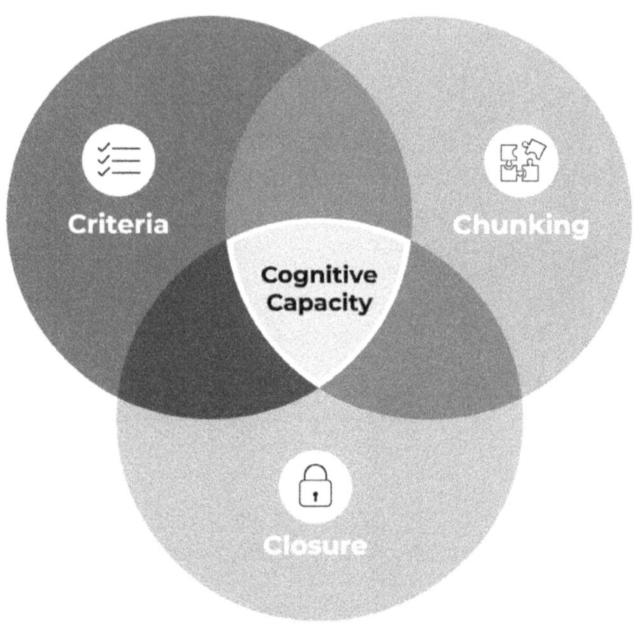

Criteria—Choosing What Deserves Attention

Criteria is about establishing the filter through which you allow information, tasks, and obligations into your system. Without criteria, everything feels equal. The urgent email, the vague request, the genuine opportunity, the trivial distraction—all carry the same weight. And so your day becomes reactive, determined by whoever shouts loudest.

I once worked with a senior leader who was drowning in initiatives. She had thirty-seven active projects listed on her wall. When I asked her which ones mattered most, she paused. "Well, all of them are important," she said. But pressed further, she admitted that only a handful aligned with her actual goals. The rest were legacy projects, nice-to-haves, or tasks she had inherited out of guilt. Without clear criteria, everything had slipped in.

Criteria is the antidote to that drift. It's the intentional act of defining what deserves space in your head and what doesn't. Think back to the supermarket. Imagine walking in without a shopping list. You wander, grab whatever looks appealing, and you end up with a trolley full of snacks and no milk. But with criteria—a list, a plan, a filter—you know what to pick up and what to leave behind. The shelves don't change. What changes is your ability to choose.

Research supports this. Psychologists Sheena Iyengar and Mark Lepper found in their famous "jam experiment" that when shoppers were offered twenty-four varieties of jam, they were less likely to buy any than when offered just six. With fewer options offered, 30% of shoppers bought jam. With twenty-four varieties, only 3% left with a jar of jam. Too much choice without criteria leads to paralysis.

Criteria restore clarity. Criteria doesn't eliminate abundance, and we can never get rid of the abundance that surrounds us. It helps you engage with that abundance without drowning in it. It's the first step to creating capacity because it protects your attention from being hijacked by everything at once.

Chunking—Working with the Brain

If Criteria is about deciding what deserves attention, Chunking is about deciding how to work with it. About how to help your brain process quicker and more effectively—to help your brain make sense of the world by supporting its capacity and way of working. The brain doesn't process every piece of information individually. It groups, it categorises, it compresses. That's why you can remember a phone number as "0400/123/456" instead of "0-4-0-0-1-2-3-4-5-6." Chunking is the brain's way of conserving energy.

In practice, chunking means grouping related tasks, structuring information, and working in blocks instead of fragments. It's about reducing cognitive switching costs by packaging things together.

I once coached a project manager who was constantly frazzled. Her day looked like a patchwork quilt: half an hour on one project, five minutes on an email, ten minutes on a call, fifteen minutes fixing a report, then back to the first project. She was exhausted, not because she wasn't skilled, but because she was context-switching dozens of times a day. When we reorganised her workload into chunks—dedicating mornings to deep project work, afternoons to meetings, and a short block to administrative tasks—her stress dropped. The same volume of work became more manageable because it was structured in alignment with how the brain prefers to process.

Cognitive Load Theory (Sweller, 1988) explains this. Our working memory has a limited capacity, but chunking reduces the burden. Instead of holding ten separate facts, the brain holds one pattern. Instead of juggling ten balls, you juggle three bundles.

Chunking also explains why experts can handle more complexity than novices. A chess grandmaster doesn't see thirty-two pieces; they see patterns and structures. Similarly, a surgeon doesn't think of every muscle and vessel individually, but as systems. Chunking allows complexity to be absorbed without overwhelming working memory.

Applied to your own life, chunking means designing your tasks and information so they are grouped, structured, and ordered. Without chunking, everything feels fragmented. With chunking, you can breathe.

Closure—Closing the Loop

Criteria help you choose what matters. Chunking helps you process it. Closure helps you release it.

The most important research to support this is by psychologist Bluma Zeigarnik, who discovered that unfinished tasks stick in the mind more than completed ones—what became known as the Zeigarnik effect. The reason is that our brains don't like open loops. When something is incomplete, it creates a subtle tension that keeps it active in working memory, nudging us until it is resolved. That's why a half-written email keeps surfacing in your thoughts, why a conversation you never followed up on nags you, or why you suddenly remember an undone task at 2am. The mind is trying to tie the thread.

Closure is about finishing loops. Not everything has to be done right now, but everything needs a resolution. That could mean completing the task, scheduling it for later, or consciously letting it go. That means closing that browser tab, document, of software program once you finished. What matters is that your brain receives a signal: this is settled.

I once worked with a communications manager who had hundreds of half-done projects. Draft newsletters, unfinished strategy docs, notes for campaigns that never launched. Each one whispered in the background: "Don't forget me." About a hundred tabs and programs open, and in her mind, it was probably the same. She felt constantly guilty, as if she were always behind.

When we created a system of closure—either finishing, filing, or formally abandoning each piece—the guilt evaporated. Her workload didn't shrink overnight, but her mental load did. The act of closure freed her capacity to focus.

Criteria, Chunking, and Closure are not independent tricks. They are interdependent. Criteria without chunking leads to clarity without progress. Chunking without closure leads to piles of half-finished bundles. Closure without criteria leads to neatness applied to the wrong things. Together, they form a cycle of capacity:

- Criteria filter what enters.
- Chunking structures what remains.
- Closure finishes and releases.

This cycle doesn't create more hours in the day. It creates more usable bandwidth in your mind. It reduces the circus acts running at once and gives you back command of the stage.

At their intersections sit deeper qualities—Meaningful, Methodical, Manageable—which we'll explore briefly now and in detail in later sections of the book.

The Intersections—Meaningful, Methodical, Manageable

The whole is greater than the sum of its parts.

—**Aristotle**

The three Cs are powerful on their own, but the real strength comes in how they intersect. Where two principles overlap, something richer emerges. These are the three Ms: Meaningful, Methodical, and Manageable.

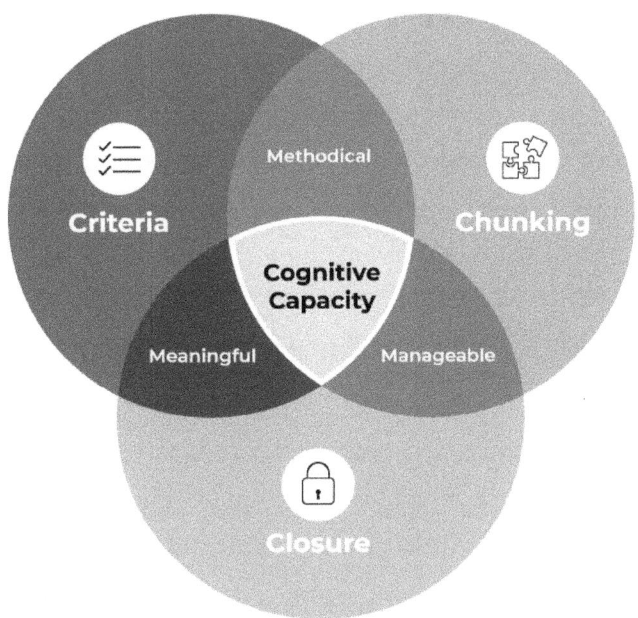

Meaningful—The Link Between Criteria and Closure

When you're clear on what matters (Criteria) and disciplined about finishing loops (Closure), you create meaning. Meaning doesn't come from doing more—it comes from aligning choices with intentions and carrying them through to completion.

Think of a martial arts student who shows up to class. She has to decide why she's there (Criteria)—to build confidence, learn discipline, or simply get fitter. And then she has to finish the class, bow out, and take that learning into her life (Closure). The meaning isn't in the isolated punches and kicks. It's in the arc from intention to completion.

Too often, our work loses meaning because we start without clarity or finish without closure. A half-written strategy, a vague initiative, a goal that drifts without result—these don't just waste effort, they erode meaning. Motivation research (Ryan & Deci's self-determination theory) shows that humans crave autonomy, competence, and relatedness. Meaning arises when we feel our actions connect with our values, build our skills, and strengthen our ties to others. Criteria and closure are the practical levers that make this happen based on the very deliberate choices we make.

Methodical—The Link Between Criteria and Chunking

Methodical work is structured, deliberate, and repeatable. It emerges when Criteria and Chunking align. You know what deserves attention, and you group and process it systematically. You are well prepared.

At work, methodical systems keep professionals sane. The project manager who stops switching every ten minutes and instead groups tasks by theme. The leader who doesn't chase every idea but organises them into strategic categories. The person who stops firefighting and starts planning.

Without methodical design, even good criteria fail. You may know what matters, but approach it chaotically. That's why methodical habits—checklists, templates, routines—aren't boring. They are capacity protectors. They provide your brain with scaffolding, so it doesn't have to reinvent every process.

Manageable—The Link Between Chunking and Closure

The third intersection is about manageability. It happens when you not only group work (Chunking) but also finish and release it

(Closure). The conscious act of supporting your brain to work with you rather than against what you need.

A communications manager once showed me her files: dozens of drafts, started but never finished. Campaign ideas half-written, proposals half-formed. She was chunking—grouping ideas—but without closure, the chunks became clutter.

Manageability comes when each chunk is carried through to a point of resolution. Instead of fifty drafts, she narrowed them down to five complete projects, finished them, and moved on. Her stress didn't come from too much creativity. It came from too little closure.

Manageable work feels lighter. It doesn't mean easy; it means proportionate. A manageable workload is one where the pieces are coherent, the chunks are clear, and the loops are closed. This is the opposite of mental clutter, where everything is started but nothing is settled.

Why This Model Is the Solution

At this stage, you might feel a sense of relief. For three chapters, we've explored the weight of overload, the saboteurs, the limits of the brain. Now, finally, here's a system that points toward lightness.

The three Cs and three Ms don't give you more hours. They don't magically erase complexity. They don't take away your workload. And they also don't take away annoying colleagues. But they help you create filters, structures, and completions that give you back bandwidth. They align with how the brain naturally works, instead of fighting against it.

Think back to the leader with thirty-seven initiatives. When she applied Criteria, she narrowed them down to the projects that truly mattered. With Chunking, she grouped them into coherent streams. With Closure, she released or finished the ones that were draining her energy. For the first time in years, her workload felt proportionate.

This model is not another productivity hack. It's not about squeezing more into the day. It's about creating space, reducing noise, and working with the brain. It's about a useful and valuable interface between you and your environment.

Now that we've covered the core principles of the filter framework, we'll dive more into how to put it into practice. In Parts II and III of the book, we'll walk through each C and each M in detail. For now, the important thing is to see the shape of the solution: that capacity is created, not wished for.

By filtering with Criteria, grouping with Chunking, and finishing with Closure, you create a foundation. By linking them into Meaningful, Methodical, and Manageable, you build depth. This model is the scaffolding that holds against overload.

Ask Yourself:

- Do I mistake being responsive for being responsible?
- How often do I feel "busy" without being clear on what actually moved forward?
- If I'm honest, where am I complicit in my own overload because I haven't drawn or enforced clear boundaries?
- What is important to me today? And what do I need?

PART II

CREATING COGNITIVE CAPACITY

CHAPTER 5

CRITERIA—DEFINING WHAT MATTERS

Everyone is always right based on their own experience.

—SETH GODIN

PART I laid our foundation in our journey to overcome information overload. We named what productivity really is (capacity, not just time and tasks). We felt the weight of overload and saw the saboteurs that eat bandwidth. We acknowledged the limits of working memory and attention. If PART I was diagnosis, PART II is design. We begin with the first lever of creating capacity: criteria.

Criteria is simply the answer to two deceptively small questions: What deserves my attention? What does not? Left implicit, those questions are answered by other people's urgency, default settings, and your own moment-to-moment mood. Made explicit, they become the prefilter that decides what gets through the door in the first place. You cannot sort everything once it's inside; that's how clutter forms. Capacity starts at the threshold. This chapter is about making that threshold real and visible in daily work. We'll start with the filter you already use (even if you can't see it), then move to the force that sharpens it: intent.

The Invisible Filter

Where you point your eyes is what you will see.

—**Naval Ravikant**

Every brain runs on a hidden triage system. In any given second, your senses are flooded with far more information than you could ever hope to process—estimates put it at around 11 million bits per second. Yet your conscious mind can handle only a sliver of that load: about 40 to 50 bits per second. The rest never reaches awareness.

This figure comes from the work of psychologist Timothy Wilson, in *Strangers to Ourselves: Discovering the Adaptive Unconscious* (2002), drawing on earlier research by Nisbett and Wilson (1977). It illustrates a profound truth: Most of what your brain does is invisible to you. Non-conscious systems do the heavy lifting—regulating your body, scanning your surroundings, filtering sensory input—so your conscious attention doesn't collapse under the weight.

Think of standing in a busy city square. Your senses are hit by colours, traffic noise, fragments of conversation, smells of food, and the feel of air on your skin. Eleven million bits per second flood in, but your awareness narrows down to the one thing that matters:

spotting your friend waving across the street. The brain's triage system discards almost everything else. Without this filtration, you'd be paralysed by noise.

This constant filtering is not just protective—it is essential.

The mind needs to filter. It chooses. It edits. It decides what gets the spotlight and what stays in the dark. Most of the time, that filtering happens without your permission. That's why two people can sit in the same meeting and leave with different stories. One heard risk; the other heard opportunity. One saw a red flag; the other saw a green light. Nothing mystical is going on. Their filters are tuned to different signals. But it also determines how you see the world. What gets through to conscious attention determines the reality you live in. We all experience a different slice of reality.

Think of it like maps. Maps are powerful—but only because they leave things out. A map does not give you everything. It's a simplified, abstracted version of reality designed to help you navigate without overwhelming you. If you included every tree, building, and blade of grass, it wouldn't be useful—it would be the size of the landscape itself.

Likewise, your mental model is a compressed version of how you understand the world. It helps you make quick decisions—but it's never the full picture. Your brain uses these internal maps to filter what's relevant, predict what might happen, and steer decisions. Just like you wouldn't use a tourist map to sail across the ocean, you shouldn't rely on the same mental model for every decision. You need to know when your map is outdated, too general, or just plain wrong.

That is why setting criteria and building your awareness of your internal operating system (your mental models) is so critical. Your brain is already filtering automatically, but without conscious criteria, the filters are crude. You risk letting in noise while missing what matters. Criteria act like an upgrade to the triage system, telling your brain: this is what to look for, this is what to ignore. Mental models add structure, so instead of treating each bit of input as random, your brain can slot it into patterns that make sense.

Here's how this plays out on an ordinary workday. You open your inbox. Dozens of messages, some important, some noise. Without an explicit filter, you default to probably one of the following ones:

- **Latest-first**—you handle the newest thing because it's on top.
- **Loudest-first**—you handle whatever looks urgent (caps, exclamation, sender status).
- **Easiest-first**—you take the quick wins to feel momentum.

Each has a logic—none has a strategy. Latest-first is nothing more than random chance. Loudest-first rewards poor boundaries and those who "scream" the loudest. Easiest-first produces a busy day that moves little that matters. The invisible filter becomes a silent boss, and you obey.

A senior manager once told me she felt "haunted" by her day. She wasn't failing—she was responsive, visible, across everything—but at 5.30pm, she couldn't answer a simple question: what did you move that mattered? Her filter was invisible and therefore unaccountable. When we pulled it into the light, two patterns appeared: she started most days by clearing small items (easiest-first) and jumped at anything marked urgent (loudest-first). None of that aligned with what her role existed to do. Nothing changed in her workload when we made the filter explicit. Her day did.

Selective attention research explains why this matters. The mind cannot attend to everything at once, so it compresses reality into a manageable stream. At any moment, your attention functions like a spotlight—illuminating one part of the stage while leaving the rest in shadow. What you notice is largely determined by what you are prepared to notice, which is why two people in the same situation can walk away with entirely different impressions.

One of the most famous demonstrations of this is the "invisible gorilla" experiment, first run by psychologists Daniel Simons and Christopher Chabris in the late 1990s. Participants were asked to watch a short video of people passing basketballs back and forth and to count the number of passes made by the team in white shirts. In the middle of the video, a person in a gorilla suit strolls through the scene, pauses, beats their chest, and walks off. You would think no one could miss it. Yet about half of the participants never noticed the gorilla at all.

The result wasn't due to stupidity—it was due to inattentional blindness. When the filter says "track the passes," the brain excludes everything else, even something as absurdly obvious as a gorilla in the middle of the frame. The experiment has since been replicated in many forms: people miss clowns riding unicycles, unexpected signs, even a person they had just spoken to moments earlier, if their attention is directed elsewhere. The question isn't whether you filter; it's whether your filter is fit for purpose.

A CFO I coached had a reputation for answering emails at lightning speed. People loved him for it; he hated himself for it.

He perceived everything important, and all of that communication-based workload required his brain—and his team wasn't growing because he was always available. When we made his criteria explicit—"strategy and people first, operations last; escalate only with a clear decision question; I don't read FYIs"—two things happened: the stream slowed, and the stream improved. He didn't become unhelpful; he became selective. The culture shifted with him.

The practical definition of criteria, then, is this: a small set of explicit rules that determine what earns attention now, what can wait, and what never enters. Invisible filters are comfortable because they absolve you of choice. Explicit criteria ask you to choose, and choice implies responsibility. That's the point. Remember this: the mind always filters; criteria decide whether it filters on purpose.

Situational Awareness

It's human nature to make the complex manageable and determine things that fit our conclusions. That's bias.

—**GEORGE BERNARD SHAW**

Consider this: 88% of human error isn't caused by bad decisions—it's caused by misreading the situation. Situational awareness is the process by which our brain makes sense of the world in real time. Endsley's model is a foundational concept in cognitive systems and human performance, particularly in high-stakes environments like aviation, healthcare, and military operations. It outlines how individuals understand and respond to their environment in three key stages: the better this system runs, the sharper your judgment. The worse it runs, the more likely you'll be overwhelmed, miss cues, or default to outdated models. Situational awareness is deeply subjective, influenced by stress, bias, inexperience, and limited cognitive capacity. Think back to the ten saboteurs as mentioned earlier in Chapter 3. The more cluttered your input or fixed your mindset, the more distorted the picture.

1. **Perception**—noticing the relevant cues in your environment (e.g., the unread emails, the tone in someone's voice, a change in project scope).
2. **Comprehension**—making sense of those cues by linking them to what you already know (your mental models).
3. **Projection**—anticipating what will happen next and preparing an appropriate response.

Most children of my generation grew up with *the* model of "womanhood" and that was Barbie—perfect hair, always smiling, and the hips (a humanly impossible figure). The same goes for fairy tales with the "happily ever after" close of the story. As an adult, these imprints have a profound, albeit subconsciously, impact on your thinking. It's like an unspoken standard you never really challenge. That's the danger of poor situational awareness: we project previous knowledge onto a current situation.

Criteria is all about the preselection and filtering of what matters. It's the cognitive sieve that lets the right things in, before you even begin to process or decide. Let's map that to Endsley's stages:

1. **Perception** = filtering input (Criteria at work!).

Criteria help reduce additional load—the irrelevant, noisy, non-actionable information. With strong criteria, you're not trying to perceive everything—you're perceiving what matters.

2. Comprehension = matching input to mental models.

Once you've perceived the right things, comprehension is about interpretation. If your criteria are fuzzy or missing, you'll misinterpret the signal—or worse, never notice it.

3. Projection = acting with intention.

Projection—the ability to anticipate consequences—is only possible when the previous two stages are clean. If you're taking in irrelevant info or misinterpreting it, your predictions will be flawed.

The challenge is to bring situational awareness into the light. Ask: what am I perceiving? What am I blind to? In a noisy world, this reflection can feel like a luxury. It isn't. It's setting your own new standards in an overloaded world.

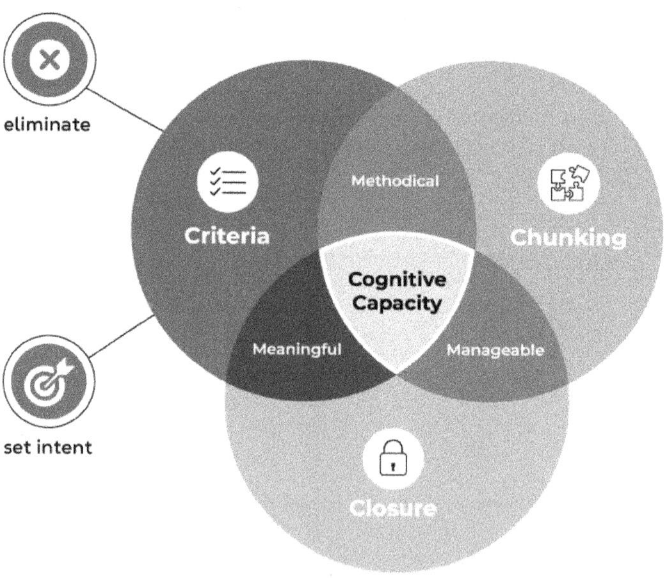

Set Intent

Deciding what not to do is as important as deciding what to do.

—STEVE JOBS

Intention is the force that sharpens criteria. Without intent, criteria become slogans. With intent, they become commitments. Think of intent as your aim. It answers a deeper question than "what first?" It goes beyond prioritisation. It asks, "What's important to me right now?" Most of us, especially when under pressure, often forget that we are allowed to ask that question.

I recently tested for third-degree black belt. So obviously, that is a big thing for Eve Broenland Kyo Sa Nim (that's my instructor title), the martial artist side of me. I've been training for many years, preparing for many months, and now it was go time. I practice a Korean karate-style called Soo Bahk Do, and it's a big part of my life; I run the school with my husband, who has been my instructor since we met at martial arts training back in the Netherlands twenty-two years ago. It obviously means a lot to me, but I also have many other commitments. How I used intent for the grading was through very environmentally focused choices, so the boundaries were evident; this weekend, only the grading mattered.

- I had no other commitments in the calendar from Friday afternoon to Tuesday morning (yes, I even blocked out Monday as a day to recover!).

- I planned out all the meals in advance so I know we'll eat well (and something to look forward to on the way home when I'm utterly exhausted).
- I built a morning routine for the Saturday and Sunday to mindfully get ready and prepare my body (let's get through this without injuries).

Intent looks ordinary in daily work: Small moves, big consequences. You stop letting the environment dictate your aim. You aim yourself. Setting an intention isn't about adding another task to your morning routine. It's about creating an anchor—a quiet decision about how you want to show up, regardless of what the day throws at you. It's small, but mighty.

In practice, this might look like:

- Beginning the day by naming the three outcomes that would make it meaningful.
- Asking "why me, why now?" before accepting an invitation.
- Rewriting a vague request into a concrete decision question before you start.
- Choosing one role to inhabit for the next hour—creator, reviewer, leader—rather than trying to be all three at once.

There's a cognitive reason why intent helps. Decision fatigue is real. Each micro-choice—open, reply, forward, accept, schedule—consumes a little fuel. When intent is clear, you batch those choices under a single heading: today I move X. Choices become expressions of direction rather than isolated problems to solve. The brain, which loves patterns and hates ambiguity, relaxes into a groove.

There's also an emotional reason. Intention reclaims agency. One of the most corrosive feelings in overloaded work is learned helplessness—the sense that events happen to you and your job is to absorb them. When you carry intent, you rewrite that contract. You won't control everything, but you will control what your attention is meant for.

For a concrete example, a project manager set the following daily intent: "move the project." Not "work on the project" (too vague), not "deal with email" (too broad). Move it. That single verb became the filter. During the day, her decisions aligned with it: which meetings to shorten, which email threads to step out of, which document to push to a decision. She still attended to email. She still sat in meetings. But her attention served a direction, and by 4pm, she could notice the progress.

Here's how intent can help you, too.

You probably will feel resistance initially. Your default approach protected you from the discomfort of choosing. Explicit intent removes that shield. You will worry about being less helpful, less available, and less good. Call that feeling what it is: withdrawal from an addiction to indiscriminate yes. You are not becoming less generous; you are becoming more truthful about what your role exists to do.

- Make it tangible or visible. Write it on a Post-it is the simplest way (and it serves as a great reminder).
- When you get distracted (and you will!), it's easier to get back to your focus because of your intentional decision.
- Intent will channel your focus (it simplifies); you'll be surprised how much more you'll get done today.

- It will also help you with boundaries; it's easier to say no when you know what your "yes" is.

Clients often ask me, "What if my boss doesn't like it, that they feel I'm not available or pushing back?" Good question. Two thoughts. First, leaders are more anxious about ambiguity than about boundaries. When you bring a crisp aim and clear criteria, you reduce their risk. Second, intent should be declared with context, not defiance. "Here's what my week is for. If something threatens that, let's solve it together."

One last story to close this section. A team I worked with adopted a ritual called opening directions. Mondays at 9.05am, each person stated a one-sentence intent out loud. Not a list; an aim. "Create the onboarding checklist." "Review marketing analytics." "Build Q3 report framework." They all wrote those sentences down to mark their intent. In stand-ups, the question changed from "What did you do?" to "What moved the aim?" The week felt lighter, not because there was less to do, but because more of what they did pointed the same way.

Eliminate

If it's not a clear yes, it's a clear no.

—GREG MCKEOWN

Criteria are not only about choosing; they are about excluding. It is tempting to think of filters as gentle guides that help us pick what matters. But in practice, the sharper edge of Criteria is elimination—the courage to say no, to shut doors, to enforce boundaries.

Think of a cockpit. Every dial, switch, and screen is there for a reason. But pilots aren't staring at hundreds of readouts simultaneously. Instruments are grouped, sequenced, and layered so that in any given moment, only the most relevant data is foregrounded. If everything shouted equally, the result would be paralysis. The cockpit works because irrelevant information is hidden, suppressed, or collapsed into summary signals. That is what allows pilots to make decisions under pressure. The same logic applies to knowledge work. When everything is visible—emails, drafts, to-do lists, requests— nothing is clear.

The brain, however, resists elimination. Cognitive biases conspire against it, such as:

- **The Endowment Effect:** We overvalue what we already have, simply because it's ours. That half-finished report feels too "valuable" to delete, even though it will never be finished.
- **Loss Aversion:** Losing something hurts about twice as much as gaining something comparable feels good. Deleting a file feels like giving up, even if it clears space.
- **FOMO:** The fear that saying no now means missing the one opportunity that might have mattered keeps our calendars and inboxes bloated.

These biases show up everywhere. We keep "just in case" documents we'll never use. We hang on to outdated processes because abandoning them feels like a waste. We hoard emails as if they are insurance against forgetting. We say yes to meetings we shouldn't attend, worried that absence means irrelevance. The result is not preparedness—it is cognitive hoarding. Every unnecessary item left in the system steals clarity, occupies mental real estate, and weakens capacity.

Elimination is the antidote. It is the discipline of deciding.

If this does not fit my intent, it goes. Not later. Not maybe. Now. This doesn't mean recklessness or indifference. It means acknowledging that space is as valuable as substance. An empty calendar slot is not wasted—it is reclaimed attention. A trimmed inbox is not a loss—it is regained focus.

Consider decluttering a wardrobe. At first, every item feels justifiable: "I might wear this someday." Then you create criteria: Have I worn it in a year? Does it fit my life now? Suddenly, the decision sharpens. Most of the wardrobe leaves, and the relief is visceral. The same applies to your digital and cognitive wardrobes. Without criteria, everything lingers. With criteria, the load lightens.

Elimination feels harsh. In truth, it is mercy. Mercy for your future self, who no longer carries invisible debt. Mercy for your team, who can see what matters. Mercy for your capacity, which finally gets to stretch. Clarity is rarely about adding more. It is about subtracting the noise that disguises itself as value.

Expectations

Expectations are resentments waiting to happen.

—Anne Lamott

If criteria are filters, expectations are the invisible presets. They determine what you count as "enough," "success," or "normal." Often, they were installed long ago—by parents, teachers, bosses, or culture—and never updated. They are like your own personal biases. And they are not helpful. Time to examine and let go.

Expectations can run like outdated software in the background, shaping your decisions without your awareness. You work late, not because today requires it, but because somewhere you absorbed the rule that "committed people stay visible after hours." You overprepare a presentation, not because the audience needs detail, but because your self-worth is tied to perfection. This is why Brené Brown warns that "disappointment is unmet expectations, and the more significant the expectations, the more significant the disappointment." If you never examined the criteria behind those expectations, you will carry guilt for standards you didn't even choose.

Workplaces magnify this. A team assumes "ASAP" means hours, not days. A leader assumes "update me" means weekly, not monthly. Expectations unspoken become criteria enforced by accident.

The way forward is not to erase expectations but to audit them. Which criteria are mine? Which were inherited? Which serve my role today, and which are ghosts from a past context?

A manager once confessed she felt "behind" if she left the office before 6pm. Her work was done, her outcomes solid, her team thriving. We unpacked the expectation. It wasn't her boss—it was her father, who commended visible hard work. The filter was invisible, but the cost was real: hours lost, resentment growing. Once she saw it, she rewrote the rule. She left on time. Nothing broke. Everything improved. Expectations are criteria in disguise. Left hidden, they distort. Brought into light, they can be chosen.

In Closing

Criteria is the first "C" because it defines the battlefield. Without it, you fight everywhere at once. With it, you fight where it matters. We've seen the invisible filter at work, how intent sharpens it, how situational awareness shapes it, how elimination enforces it, and how expectations silently guide it.

Strong criteria do not guarantee capacity. But without them, capacity is impossible. They are the gateway. Everything else follows. As we move to the next chapter—Chunking—we'll see what happens once the right things are inside. Criteria decide what gets through. Chunking decides how to hold them without collapse.

Action Steps:

1. **Be clear on your criteria.** Before you start your day, before you attend that meeting, before you come home—ask yourself, "What's important to me?" or "What's my intent/aim/objective?" It'll make all the difference.

2. **If the situation allows, communicate your intent.** Those around you might find it helpful, or they can support you. And even the act of stating it out loud will help you anchor in your intent and help you stay on course.

3. **Eliminate the rest.** Don't keep those options open or let them take up cognitive capacity by saying to yourself, "Just in case, I'll keep this." Set intent.

4. **Question the expectations** you feel are put on yourself, by yourself, or by others.

Ask Yourself:

- What's the first thing I usually say "yes" to without thinking—and how often does it actually deserve that yes?
- Which "shoulds" in my head sound suspiciously like someone else's voice?
- What's one small thing I keep doing out of habit that, if I stopped, no one would actually notice?
- If I gave my day a title—like a book chapter—what would it be today: "Running Around," "Moving Things Forward," or "Lost in the Inbox"?
- If my calendar reflected only what I decided truly mattered, how different would it look?

CHUNKING—SMARTER PROCESSING

In the last chapter, we explored criteria—the conscious filters that let you decide what gets through the door of your attention. Without them, you drown in input. With them, you reclaim a measure of control. But criteria alone are not enough. Even once you've set your intent and eliminated the irrelevant, what remains can still overwhelm.

Imagine a colleague hands you a box full of loose Lego bricks. No instruction sheet, no containers, just thousands of pieces of every shape and colour. The bricks themselves might be valuable, but without a system to sort and assemble them, they are almost useless. Now imagine the same bricks sorted by type, colour, and size, and grouped into bags that match the building steps. Suddenly, possibility appears. That is the difference between raw input and organised chunks.

This is where the second "C" of creating cognitive capacity comes in: Chunking. Where criteria are about choosing, chunking is about holding. It is how you reduce complexity into something the mind can carry without buckling. Without chunking, every email, request, and thought weighs the same—like juggling ten balls in the air at once. With chunking, you collapse those ten into two or three patterns you can hold, name, and move forward.

Chunking: The Brain's Way of Turning Chaos into Clarity

By organizing information into meaningful patterns, we reduce mental effort.

—JOHN SWELLER, COGNITIVE LOAD THEORY

Psychologists have known for decades that working memory is astonishingly small. In the 1950s, George Miller proposed his famous law: The mind can hold about seven items at once, plus or minus two. Later research refined that number downward; in practice, the bandwidth is closer to four. Think about that: Of the millions of bits you encounter every second, only a handful can be active in your conscious mind at any given time.

This bottleneck is not a flaw. It is the design. Working memory forces you to compress, to simplify, to prioritise. If you couldn't, you would be paralysed by detail.

Chunking is the brain's workaround for this bottleneck. By grouping bits of information into meaningful patterns, you increase what can be held. A simple example: Remembering the sequence "1-9-4-5-2-0-2-4" as eight digits is hard. But if you chunk it as "1945" and "2024," it becomes two items, not eight. The capacity hasn't changed; the efficiency has.

We rely on this constantly. You don't think of every letter in a word, every word in a sentence, or every key on a keyboard. You chunk them: syllables, phrases, muscle memory. Expert chess players recall board positions, not because they have photographic memory but because they recognise patterns—chunks—that compress complexity. This is why learning feels heavy at first and light later. Beginners must hold every piece separately. Experts see the same scene as a handful of chunks. The difference is not raw intelligence but practised grouping.

In daily work, the same dynamic applies. Without chunking, every email feels like a brand-new demand, every meeting like a fresh puzzle, every idea like an isolated weight. The brain ends up juggling dozens of tiny, disconnected fragments. With chunking, you reduce the noise into categories you can actually carry: "client concerns," "team dynamics," "strategic risks." Suddenly, instead of holding twenty open loops, you're holding three coherent buckets. The work hasn't changed, but your cognitive load has.

The research is clear. Cognitive Load Theory, developed by educational psychologist John Sweller, shows that humans learn and perform best when information is grouped in ways that align with the strict limits of working memory. Raw fragments overload the system and cause it to fail; organised chunks allow comprehension, pattern recognition, and problem-solving. This is why you remember phone numbers better when they're grouped into three sets of digits, or why musicians memorise complex pieces as phrases rather than individual notes. The brain isn't built to hold endless fragments—it's built to work with patterns.

Psychologist Sophie Leroy's work on attention residue adds another layer. When we switch tasks, part of our attention remains stuck on the unfinished work. It's like leaving tabs open in the background of your mind—slowing performance, draining focus, and leaving you scattered. Chunking reduces this leakage. By grouping similar tasks and staying in one mental mode longer, you allow your attention to settle rather than fragment. Answering emails in a batch, for example, creates less residue than darting in and out between emails, strategy documents, and quick chats.

The benefit is not only efficiency but also energy conservation. Switching modes constantly forces the brain to reconfigure its mental set—like asking a runner to stop and change shoes every hundred meters. Chunking creates continuity, which protects energy for deeper work.

Context-switching is mentally exhausting and drains your cognitive capacity.

And there's a deeper psychological payoff: chunking restores a sense of progress. Instead of feeling perpetually unfinished—twenty tasks half-started—you experience progress in batches: "I cleared the client concerns," "I finished the team dynamics issues." Progress feels tangible, and with it comes motivation.

Context-switching is
mentally exhausting and
drains your cognitive
capacity.

Chunking isn't just about grouping tasks; it also shapes how we process meaning. Psycholinguistic research on semantic priming (Meyer & Schvaneveldt, 1971) shows that when people read a passage about medicine, they recognise words like *doctor* and *nurse* more quickly than unrelated simple words like *cat*. Why? Because the brain activates an existing schema—a mental "chunk" of related concepts—and processes everything inside that chunk faster. Once the medical frame is triggered, associated ideas are easier to retrieve, interpret, and connect.

The same happens in daily work. When you group related tasks together—say, reviewing all team communication in one block— you activate a mental set that speeds recognition and reduces strain. Instead of treating each email or request as a separate puzzle, you're drawing from a prepared chunk, and the mind works more fluidly.

Anecdotes confirm what science explains. A client once described her brain as a thousand Post-its stuck inside her skull. Every task, every worry, every unfinished thing competed for space. We worked on grouping them into just four categories aligned with her role: strategy, people, operations, and personal. Suddenly, she didn't have a thousand Post-its. She had four buckets. She could breathe again.

Chunking, then, is not a small organisational trick. It's a structural way of working with the brain's natural design rather than against it. It takes the fragmented input of modern work and reshapes it into patterns the mind can carry, comprehend, and complete. It speeds up our mental processing.

Why does this matter for cognitive capacity? Because without chunking, your brain gets overloaded much quicker. Your brain becomes a crowded hallway with no filing system. With chunking, you create containers that free bandwidth for deeper work.

Effective Information Processing

Structure doesn't restrict freedom. It creates it.

—Jocko Willink

Criteria decide what enters. Chunking decides what happens next. The first move is to transform noise into information. Psychologists describe this as a ladder:

- **Noise:** Raw, unfiltered input. Slack pings, random headlines, irrelevant chatter.
- **Data:** Signals structured enough to be measured. Numbers, timestamps, lists.
- **Information:** Data gives context and meaning. A sales number compared to last quarter.
- **Knowledge:** Information integrated into understanding and applied to our decisions.

Without chunking, you get stuck in noise. Or worse, you drown in data without making it meaningful. We see this instinctively when driving in an unfamiliar neighbourhood. To find the right house, you often turn down the music. Why? Because the extra noise clutters working memory.

Other research adds weight. Neuroscientists Adam Gazzaley and Larry Rosen, in *The Distracted Mind*, show that task-switching doesn't just slow us down—it fractures the way we process information. Each time you toggle between unrelated streams—say, pausing mid-spreadsheet to answer a text, then skimming your inbox before hopping back to numbers—you force your brain to tear down one mental frame and build another from scratch. What feels like a smooth multitasking dance is, in reality, a series of costly resets.

Think of it like climbing a ladder. When you're focused, you move steadily upward: noise becomes data, data becomes information, information becomes knowledge. But each interruption yanks you back down. You don't just pause at your current rung—you tumble two or three rungs lower and must rebuild context before climbing again. This is why a "quick check of email" can consume twenty minutes of lost momentum.

Psychologists call this "switching cost," and the numbers are sobering. Research from Gloria Mark at the University of California, Irvine, found it takes an average of twenty-three minutes to return to the same level of focus after an interruption. That means a single Teams chat, Slack ping, or calendar notification doesn't just steal seconds—it taxes nearly half an hour of cognitive recovery.

Chunking is the antidote. By grouping similar tasks, you reduce the number of context shifts. If you process emails in a single batch, your mind stays in "communication mode." If you schedule all your one-on-one meetings back-to-back, you stay in "conversation mode." It's the same reason chefs prep ingredients in batches before cooking. Chopping all the onions at once is easier than switching between chopping, sautéing, boiling, and then chopping again.

Stories from high-stakes environments make the point vivid. Air traffic controllers manage dozens of planes at once, but they don't treat each aircraft as a separate mental puzzle. They chunk them— by altitude, approach pattern, or runway assignment. Without that grouping, the constant switching would overwhelm even the best-trained minds. Surgeons do the same: they sequence procedures into stages so the team can stay in one cognitive mode at a time rather than scattering attention across dozens of simultaneous demands.

In ordinary work, the principle is just as powerful. One manager I coached resisted chunking because he liked to "stay responsive." But his days dissolved into a blur of context shifts. We tried a simple experiment: instead of answering every email as it arrived, he created two 30-minute windows each day for replies. Within a week, his sense of control returned.

The economics of scarcity offer another angle. Mullainathan and Shafir's *Scarcity* describes the "bandwidth tax": when cognitive load is high, we tunnel on the immediate at the cost of the important. Poor farmers under financial strain perform worse on cognitive tests—not because they are less intelligent, but because scarcity hijacks their bandwidth. Overloaded workers do the same with time: they tunnel on urgent noise, not meaningful knowledge. Chunking is the mental design principle that lifts you out of the tunnel.

Journalist Johann Hari captures the danger of not chunking in *Stolen Focus*. He argues that our culture is flooded with fractured signals—notifications, algorithm-driven feeds, clickbait headlines—that keep us permanently at the level of noise. Without deliberate chunking, our minds never climb to knowledge. We stay scattered, reactive, and consumptive. Hari describes talking to Silicon Valley designers who openly admitted their platforms were engineered to exploit our attentional weaknesses. Each notification is not neutral—it's a hook designed to pull you back into the feed. Every alert, every "ding," every red bubble is a demand to reset your cognitive ladder, tumbling you back to noise. It isn't that you lack willpower. It's that you are swimming in an environment optimised for distraction.

The numbers are staggering. Research by RescueTime, a productivity software company, shows the average worker checks email or messaging tools every six minutes. Many never experience more than five consecutive minutes of uninterrupted focus. That isn't a quirk of personality—it's the architecture of modern work. In *A World Without Email,* Cal Newport argues that "the hyperactive hive mind" of constant communication keeps knowledge workers stuck in a perpetual first rung: dealing with messages rather than producing meaning.

The consequences aren't just lost productivity. They're lost meaning. Hari recounts how teenagers who spend more time on fractured social media streams show higher rates of anxiety and depression. Adults, too, report "brain fog" and reduced memory recall after extended bouts of digital multitasking. The brain, bombarded by fragments, loses the ability to sustain coherent thought. We consume endlessly, but we rarely integrate.

This is why deliberate chunking matters. Without it, you're at the mercy of the environment—your attention sliced into ribbons by whatever signal happens to appear. With it, you can step out of the stream long enough to regroup. You turn fractured fragments into coherent buckets, and buckets into knowledge. In a world of engineered noise, chunking becomes an act of resistance. Chunking is not an efficiency trick. It is a survival skill in an overloaded age. The world will not reduce noise for you. Your only defence is to decide how you will group it (categorise), name it (give it a label), and resist the noise.

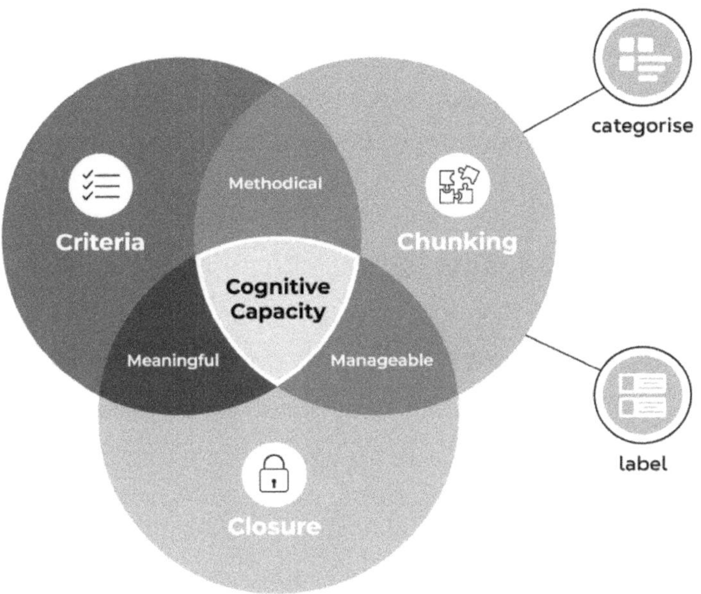

Categorise

To do two things at once is to do neither.

—**Publius Syrus**

Your brain likes order. When information is grouped together into clear categories, it's easier to store, retrieve, and act on. Without categories, everything feels urgent and jumbled—and that mental clutter makes it harder to focus, decide, and do. Categorising lets you process input faster and stay in a single mode, which preserves cognitive capacity.

Walk into any grocery store in the world and you'll find the same pattern. Milk with milk. Bread with bread. Apples beside oranges. The reason is not convenience for the shop—it's cognitive relief for the shopper. If the bread were hidden among shampoo and batteries, shopping would take hours. This is chunking at work in daily life. Categories reduce the search cost. They are externalised memory. Instead of recalling where every item might be, you recall the category, and the brain does the rest.

David Levitin, in *The Organized Mind*, explains how categories save us. Long before inboxes and spreadsheets, humans chunked the world into survival bins: edible versus poisonous plants, friend versus foe, safe versus dangerous. This wasn't optional; it was evolution's way of keeping us alive. If you had to deliberate every time you saw a berry, you'd starve before lunch. Categories were the shortcut.

Modern life simply multiplies the bins. We now sort not just berries but emails into folders, tasks into lists, music into playlists, and contacts into groups. Categorisation has scaled with civilisation. Yet the brain hasn't evolved new bandwidth in the last 40,000 years. We still work with the same four-to-seven slot working memory as our hunter-gatherer ancestors. The mismatch between ancient hardware and modern complexity is why categorisation feels both necessary and exhausting.

When categories fit, they reduce cognitive load. Categories act as externalised memory, freeing working memory for actual thinking. But when categories don't fit, they create more load than they relieve. Anyone who has stared at a bloated to-do list knows the problem. If every task lives in a single "miscellaneous" category, the list becomes noise. Likewise, too many bins splinter attention.

I once worked with a leader who had eighty-seven folders in her inbox. She spent more time deciding where an email belonged than actually answering it. Her system of categories had collapsed under its own weight. This is again decision fatigue at play. More choice doesn't equal more freedom; it equals paralysis. The same holds for your mental bins. More folders, more tags, more projects don't lighten the load—they spread it thin.

The goal, then, is not more categories but simplified and meaningful ones. A handful of well-chosen buckets that map to your real priorities. Fewer bins, better bins, smarter processing.

The alternative is cognitive hoarding—piling every input in one heap. Psychologists studying hoarders (Frost & Hartl, 1996) find that the inability to categorise (decide what belongs together and what can be discarded) is a key driver of clutter. The same applies cognitively. Without categories, everything looks urgent.

The point is not to invent categories for their own sake. It is to ask: Which categories make my life lighter? Where do I naturally group, and where do I scatter? Once you know, you can align your world to your brain rather than against it.

Label

If you can't name it, you can't tame it.

—**Brené Brown**

If categories are bins, labels are the names that make sense of them. Without a label, a bin is just a black box. With one, it becomes a tool.

Cartographers know this. A map without a legend is useless. The symbols exist, but without meaning. With a legend, the symbols tell a story: river, mountain, city, border. The same is true for your mental maps. Labels turn categories into comprehension.

I think back to a client who often said, "I feel behind." That was her label for her experience. But when we unpacked it, she wasn't actually late. She was on schedule. The real issue was her inherited expectation that she should always be "ahead." The label distorted her reality. Once she relabelled it as "progressing well," her stress reduced.

Labels also frame perception. Cognitive linguist George Lakoff has shown how political framing alters thought. Call it "tax relief," and tax is framed as a burden. Call it "investment in society," and it is framed as a contribution. The label changes what people see.

Anthropologists describe similar effects. Fascinating research by Debi Roberson points out that what we can't describe, we also can't see. The Himba Tribe in Namibia evidently can't distinguish between the colours blue and green. Not only do they not have a word to describe the colour blue, but they also can't point out a blue square surrounded by green squares. They can, however, distinguish between different shades of green a lot better than you and I can. What this tells us is that how we describe the world is how we perceive it and vice versa.

Labels create what is called cognitive fluency—the subjective ease and speed with which the mind processes information, influencing a person's perception of truth, familiarity, and confidence. So very helpful for our cognitive capacity. Psychologists have long observed that when something is easy to label, it feels truer, safer, and easier to act upon. When it's hard to label, it feels confusing or risky.

This principle applies powerfully to emotions. When you can't quite name what you feel, the emotion tends to loom larger, diffuse into everything, and feel unmanageable. But the moment you give it a label, its grip loosens.

Neuroscientist Matthew Lieberman and colleagues (2007) studied this in what is now called affect labelling. Participants were shown images of emotional faces while their brain activity was monitored with fMRI. When they were asked to name the emotion they saw—"angry," "fearful," "sad"—activity in the amygdala (the brain's alarm centre) decreased, while activity in the right ventrolateral prefrontal cortex (involved in regulation and control) increased. In other words, simply putting feelings into words dampened the intensity of the emotion and activated the brain's calming circuits.

Other research has reinforced this. Brody & Hall (2008) note that accurate labelling improves emotional regulation because it creates clarity—helping people respond with intention rather than impulse.

This matters in daily work because stress rarely announces itself clearly. It creeps up the scale (see the stress emotion scale below)—from Alert to Edgy and Uneasy to Overwhelmed—often without us noticing until we hit the upper levels. By giving each step a name, as in the stress intensity scale, we create granularity: instead of saying "I'm stressed," you can say, "I'm at level 5—tense," or "I'm at level 7—stressed but not yet anxious." This granularity is powerful. Research by Lisa Feldman Barrett (2017) in her book *How Emotions Are Made* shows that people who can label their emotions with precision cope better with stress, show greater resilience, and are less likely to spiral into anxiety or depression.

Level	Label	Description
1	Alert	Mild mental tension; aware of demands, but still steady.
2	Edgy	Slightly on edge, sensitive to interruptions or pressure.
3	Uneasy	Low-level discomfort, something feels off or uncertain.
4	Nervous	Noticeable worry or apprehension, anticipating challenges.
5	Tense	Mind and body feel tight; harder to focus or stay patient.
6	Hesitant	Doubting your capacity; starting to freeze or stall.
7	Stressed	Overloaded with tasks or thoughts, mental bandwidth strained.
8	Anxious	Strong emotional reactivity, difficulty calming thoughts or body.
9	Panicked	Urgency feels extreme; disoriented, possibly spiraling.
10	Overwhelmed	Mentally and emotionally shut down; cannot process or respond clearly.

Chunking depends on labels. Without them, categories blur. With them, categories sharpen. The work, then, is to ask: What labels am I using? Do they empower or constrain? Do they reflect today's reality or yesterday's script?

In Closing

Chunking is how you transform chaos into clarity. It helps your brain work more efficiently. It is about structuring what you carry so you can actually carry it. We saw how the brain's limits make chunking essential. We explored the relief of categories and the power of labels. Together, they form the bridge between criteria and closure. Criteria decide what gets in. Chunking decides how to hold it. Closure, which we turn to next, decides how to finish it. Chunking is cognitive hygiene, and it makes sense to not work against how your brain processes information, especially when we are overloaded.

Action Steps:

1. **Segment before you start**—group your to-dos into categories (admin, client work, writing, meetings). Identifying your modes is very helpful.

2. **Use folders/tags**—digital or physical, it doesn't matter. Use structure to make thinking faster.

3. **Batch your tasks**—block out time to perform one kind of task at once.

4. **Ask yourself what you're hoarding**—whether it's files, unread tabs, or tasks … if you can't categorise it, question whether you need it.

5. **Name your categories**—even informally. If it has a label, your brain knows where to place it.

6. **Label your emotions accurately**—don't describe a level 7 when you actually feel a 4.

Ask Yourself:

- If my inbox were a grocery store, how many aisles would it need? Too many, or too few?
- Which task mode drains you most—emails, meetings, or writing? What would chunking change?
- Which categories already exist in my life that make things easier?
- If I drew a map of my current work, what would the legend look like?
- What new label would lighten the load I'm carrying today?

CHAPTER 7

CLOSURE–CLOSE THE LOOP

Completion is not just about doing, it's about releasing.

—DAVID ALLEN

In the last chapter, we explored chunking—the way the mind reduces chaos into coherent groups so it can carry the weight of modern work. Criteria choose what gets in. Chunking helps you hold and organise it. But organising alone is not enough. What we hold must eventually be put down. That is where the third element of cognitive capacity comes in: Closure.

If chunking is about structuring the cargo mid-flight, closure is about landing the plane. Without it, we circle endlessly, carrying unresolved loops in our heads, feeling heavy without always knowing why. Closure is not just about finishing tasks—it is about giving experiences a clear boundary, an end that allows the mind to rest and reset. It's how your brain makes sense of what just happened, and gives it space to do so. It's what allows you to shift from one thing to the next with clarity and control. Without closure, your mind stays open-looped, cluttered, and reactive. In a world of overload, knowing how to close is essential.

Closure removes ambiguity, feeds your Criteria, and is a core tool for navigating our overloaded worlds. It's not just about crossing things off—it's about drawing a mental line that allows you to stop carrying the cognitive weight.

Mental Browser Tabs

Nothing is so fatiguing as the eternal hanging on of an uncompleted task.

—WILLIAM JAMES

Think about your internet browser. Each new tab consumes a little more memory. A handful is manageable. But as you accumulate dozens—half-read articles, forms you meant to complete, resources you might return to—the system slows. Your computer struggles not because any single tab is heavy, but because the open-endedness consumes resources. Our brains operate the same way. Every unfinished task, every unresolved conversation, every decision deferred is another mental tab. Without hitting 'close', you drain your mental battery. Closure is the act of hitting the little "x" on the tab: it stops background activity, frees up processing power, and keeps your system fast and clean.

There is a particular kind of exhaustion that doesn't come from long hours or heavy lifting. It comes from incompletion. It drains your cognitive capacity, making it an easy one to miss or skip. From half-finished projects, open loops, dangling to-dos, and the email you meant to answer but didn't. This is the fatigue William James named more than a century ago—the weariness not of work itself, but of work without closure.

You know the feeling. It's late at night, and instead of drifting to sleep, your brain replays tomorrow's unfinished report. Or you finish one meeting and, before you can absorb it, you're pulled into the next, still carrying fragments of the first. Your body is still, but your mind is cluttered with loose ends. This is not simply stress—it is the cognitive drag of things left undone.

Closure is the antidote. It is the intentional act of finishing, of giving shape and boundary to experience. Without closure, mental residue accumulates like tabs left open on a browser. With closure, you free bandwidth and regain presence.

The psychologist Bluma Zeigarnik first documented this in the 1920s. Sitting in a Viennese café, she noticed waiters easily remembered complex, unpaid orders—but forgot them as soon as the bill was settled. She went on to run experiments confirming this: students recalled unfinished tasks twice as well as completed ones. The mere act of completion closed the loop and released the memory. What Zeigarnik showed is that incompletion is sticky. It lingers not because we want it to, but because our brains are wired to hold on to what isn't finished. In a world of endless tasks, this stickiness becomes a liability. Her experiments confirmed it: unfinished tasks stick.

This insight has been weaponised in modern culture. Why does Netflix autoplay the next episode before you've finished processing the last? Why do social media platforms send "nudges" when you've left something incomplete? They are exploiting Zeigarnik's finding: the brain hates open loops. A cliffhanger forces attention because it withholds closure.

In a healthy context, this stickiness can help us finish work. In an unhealthy one, it becomes a trap, dragging our attention into loops we never meant to enter. The Zeigarnik Effect explains why one half-drafted email can weigh more than ten completed ones, or why a single unresolved conversation can consume more energy than a week of routine tasks. Unfinishedness hijacks the brain's attentional system.

David Allen, in *Getting Things Done*, calls these "open loops"—commitments we've made, large or small, that remain unresolved. An open loop can be as trivial as "replace the battery in the smoke alarm" or as consequential as "finalise the strategic plan." What matters is not the scale of the task, but its incompletion. The brain treats them with the same vigilance: something unfinished needs attention.

Allen's insight is deceptively simple: stress doesn't come from the sheer volume of work, but from the failure to close these loops. That's why you can feel strangely lighter after making a list, even if nothing is yet done. The act of writing captures the loop outside your head. It signals to the brain that the item is being handled, freeing up space.

Allen often illustrates this with the example of a nagging errand: say, buying lightbulbs. Until the task is captured in a trusted system, your brain will remind you at random times—while driving, while in bed, while in a meeting. None of these are moments when you can actually complete the task. The reminder is wasted, yet it consumes bandwidth. Multiply this across dozens of open loops, and you have the background hum of stress many professionals carry daily.

Closure interrupts this cycle. It doesn't always mean finishing the task immediately. Sometimes it means deciding when and how it will be done, and parking it in a trusted place. That act of containment closes the loop in the mind, even if the task is still pending. It's why people feel a surge of relief after a weekly review or even a short journaling session. The brain stops hoarding the loop because it recognises it is accounted for.

The logic echoes neuroscience research on working memory. Coming back to psychologist John Sweller's *Cognitive Load Theory*, it shows how limited working memory is: try juggling more than a handful of pieces of information, and performance drops sharply. Open loops inflate that load. Each unresolved task competes for attention in working memory, degrading performance across the board.

The Zeigarnik Effect explains why unfinished tasks stick in memory, but modern research shows the consequences go further. Psychologist Sophie Leroy coined the term "attention residue" to describe what happens when we leave one task incomplete and move to another. Part of our attention stays stuck on the unfinished work, which in turn reduces performance on the next. In her experiments, participants who were asked to switch tasks midstream performed worse on the new task than those allowed to finish the first task. The residue impaired focus, accuracy, and efficiency. Multiply this across a workday—half-written emails, unresolved meetings, interrupted projects—and it's clear why so many professionals feel drained without knowing why. They describe feeling "always on" but never fully present.

This is one reason why multitasking is such a myth. We are not designed to hold dozens of mental tabs open without cost. Every switch leaves a trace of residue, slowing us down, lowering quality, and consuming capacity. It's not just the volume of work. It's the lack of closure.

Closure, whether through completion or capture, restores working memory for what it does best—reasoning and creativity. This distinction is liberating. It reframes stress, not as a reflection of personal inadequacy but as a signal of unclosed loops. It suggests that the way to lighten the mind and therefore create cognitive capacity is not to "try harder" or "get motivated", but to build systems of closure. Lists, rituals, reviews, debriefs—these are not administrative chores. They are cognitive offloading devices. They are the punctuation marks that let your brain do what it is designed to do: solve, not store.

Let's find out how we can add closure to our workflow for enhanced cognitive capacity.

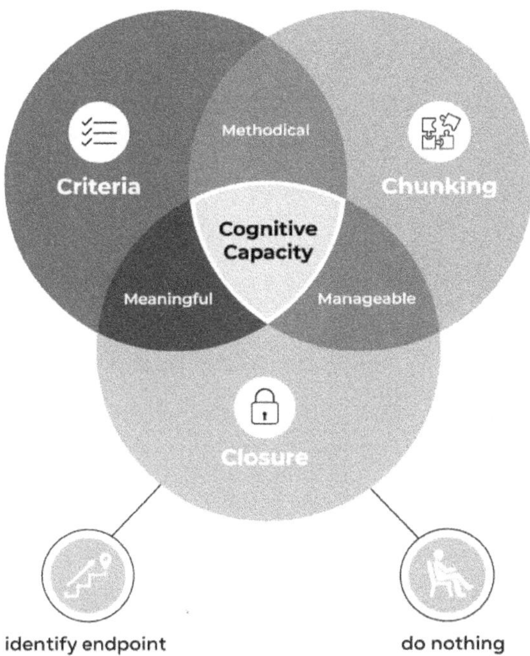

Identify Endpoint

I once worked with a team that had delivered a major project after two years of intense effort. They hit the deadline, launched the system, celebrated briefly—and then immediately shifted into "what's next?" mode. The problem was, they never closed the chapter. No proper debrief, no acknowledgement of milestones, no shared reflection on lessons learned. Six months later, morale was low. People described feeling as though they were still carrying the project, even though it was technically done. As one manager put it, "It feels like we climbed the mountain, but nobody ever said we reached the top". The team wasn't disengaged. They were unfinished. Closure was absent.

This is the hidden cost of modern work cultures that prize relentless forward motion. Without closure, teams burn out, not from effort, but from the accumulation of unresolved effort. Stop moving the goal post. If you don't have a clear endpoint to serve as an anchor for what finished looks like, your brain will never register that it's done. So the Zeigarnik Effect will continue. Having clear criteria to begin with will aid you in identifying your endpoint.

Closure is often blocked, not by external pressures but by our own habits. Maria, a senior leader I once coached, had a tendency to move her own finish line. She would complete a presentation, but before acknowledging it as done, she would add "just one more tweak." She would finish a successful event and immediately say, "Next time we'll …" without pausing to close the current chapter.

Her intentions were good—she wanted excellence (hello, perfectionists out there). But the effect was exhaustion. Neither she nor her team ever felt a sense of completion. The work was endless because the goalpost always moved. Then she began building intentional closure into her process—marking milestones, celebrating small wins, drawing lines under projects. Closure, she discovered, was not about lowering standards. It was about preserving capacity. Without it, excellence collapses into fatigue.

Doing Nothing

All men's miseries derive from not being able to sit in a quiet room alone.

—BLAISE PASCAL

Last week, I caught myself staring out into the backyard with a hot coffee in hand. No music, no scrolling, no multitasking—gosh, I even think I wasn't thinking. Just me, my breath, and a very confused puppy wondering why I wasn't doing anything (well, or at least not petting him). Ten minutes passed. And what followed: clarity. A solution to a client challenge clicked into place, an idea for this newsletter surfaced, and—most importantly—I felt better. Calmer. Sharper. More me.

In our productivity-obsessed culture, doing nothing can feel like failure, a waste of time, and highly underrated. But it's extremely vital that you learn how to do this. Before we dive into the neuroscience of why, here's a cultural insight that doing nothing is regarded as essential in many cultures. We've just forgotten how to practice it in our overloaded worlds.

- The Dutch call it *Niksen*—literally meaning doing nothing.
- The Italians call it *Dolce Far Niente*—the sweet art of doing nothing.
- The Jews have *Sabbath*—a sacred day of rest.
- The Swedes have *Hygge*—cozy, unhurried moments that restore calm and presence.
- The Japanese call it *Yutori*—which refers to a sense of spaciousness, both in time and mental state; it's about not cramming your schedule.

- The Chinese call it *Wu-Wei-Wu*—meaning actionless action, a core concept in Taoism.

The great inventor Thomas Edison was known for seeking closure in unconventional ways. After long stretches of work, he would retreat to a pond with a fishing rod. But here's the twist: he rarely baited the hook. He had no real intention of catching fish. What he sought was the ritual of ending. Fishing was his closure mechanism. By the time he returned, his mind was lighter, ready for what came next.

Alex Pang, in his book *Rest*, makes a provocative claim: the people we hold up as history's paragons of productivity were often just as disciplined about their downtime as they were about their output. Charles Darwin may have written some of the most influential scientific works in history, but he also built his days around long, deliberate walks on his "thinking path" at Down House. These weren't idle strolls. They were rituals of closure, a way to draw a line under stretches of intense study and let the mind reset before the next burst of work.

Pang's insight is that these routines weren't eccentric quirks; they were structural. They marked the boundary between effort and release, allowing energy to replenish for the next act. Without them, even geniuses would have burned out. With them, their capacity multiplied.

Celeste Headlee, in her book *Do Nothing*, warns that our culture has erased these natural punctuation marks. Instead of Darwin's walks, we fill every gap with podcasts, emails, and scrolling. Instead of disciplined separation, we collapse work and home into the same room, the same device, the same chair. Leisure itself becomes another form of work: workouts are tracked, vacations documented, and even hobbies turned into side hustles. Rest no longer restores; it performs. And the performance is never finished.

Jenny Odell takes this critique further in *How to Do Nothing*. She argues that reclaiming our attention requires more than just closing loops between tasks—it requires closing the loop on the entire system that demands constant output. Sitting in a rose garden to watch birds, as she describes, is not idleness in the trivial sense. It is an act of resistance, a conscious creation of space where nothing is demanded, nothing is measured, and nothing needs to be monetised. Doing nothing, in this view, is not wasted time. It is Closure against the culture of endlessness.

Seen together, Pang, Headlee, and Odell paint a picture of rest as active closure. Boundaries are not luxuries—they are the invisible architecture of capacity. The walks, the rituals, the empty rooms, the pauses: these were not indulgences. They were the acts that made sustained productivity possible.

Neuroscience reinforces this. The default mode network—the brain system active during rest—plays a crucial role in consolidating memory, sparking creativity, and processing emotion. But it only functions properly when the mind is not clogged with unresolved tasks. Closure clears the runway for rest. Without it, downtime becomes rumination time, and the brain never truly resets.

Now for the challenging part: actually putting this into practice. Our minds are so primed for constant activity that our environment rewards us with little happy hormones whenever we get distracted. Most people will resist doing nothing. We feel guilty or at least useless if we're not doing anything. In addition to that, if your to-do list isn't finished—how can you justify not doing anything? But you have to, for your mental well-being, your productivity, and for making it sustainable. If this concept of doing nothing freaks you out a little, I'm also happy for you to refer to it as intentional idleness. It gives a little purpose to it. But you have to give yourself permission to do nothing. Your capacity needs it.

Create a Closure Ritual

Closure is punctuation for the mind. Imagine a page without commas or full stops. The words might still be there, but the meaning is lost in the breathless rush. This is why rituals of closure matter. They are our commas, colons, and full stops. Some are formal—graduations, retirements, funerals. Others are personal—shutting the laptop with intention, writing a quick reflection at the end of the day, tidying the desk before leaving. Rituals are physical anchor points for the mind to register your endpoint. These punctuation marks are not wasted time; they are the grammar of capacity.

Cal Newport, in *Deep Work*, talks about his "shutdown ritual". Each evening, he closes his day by reviewing tasks, updating lists, and saying aloud, "shutdown complete". It might sound mechanical, but it is deeply freeing. His mind knows the day is finished. He has landed the plane, punctuated the sentence, and closed the loop. Without punctuation, both language and life collapse into incoherence. Closure provides the grammar we need to make sense of our effort.

Maya Angelou, meanwhile, was famous for renting sparse hotel rooms where she would go to write. The sterility of the space—the bare bed, the desk with only a bible, a dictionary, and a bottle of sherry—wasn't incidental. It was closure by design. When she left that room, the work stayed behind. The ritual separation gave her back her life outside the page, ensuring she wasn't endlessly carrying her manuscripts in her head.

Even Beethoven, a man synonymous with artistic obsession, understood the need for boundaries. His morning ritual was legendary: counting out exactly sixty coffee beans for his daily brew before beginning his composition. It wasn't superstition. It was punctuation. The ritual grounded him, signalled the shift into creative mode, and gave shape to the day. When he walked later in the afternoons, he wasn't just exercising—he was creating closure from the mental exertion of composing.

In Closing (great pun actually)

Closure is not indulgence; it is essential. It is what allows the mind to move freely instead of dragging a trail of unfinished weight behind it. Without closure, capacity leaks away. With it, clarity and calm return. In a culture that celebrates endless motion, choosing to finish, to punctuate, to pause—even to do nothing—is a radical act. But it is also a necessary one. Closure is not the end of productivity; it is what makes sustained productivity possible. With closure, you regain not just capacity, but yourself.

Action Steps:

1. **Have a clear endpoint.** Stop moving the goalpost midway or, even worse, near the end. Describing your tasks or projects accurately helps with this. Don't say "management report," but "review production and safety data for the monthly management report".

2. **Find out how you can start learning to do nothing.** What's going to work for you is essential to figure out. This is really hard for most people, so give yourself time to try and see how you go.

3. **Create a closure ritual.** Especially to close your working day. Bonus points for a tangible, physical process.

Ask Yourself:

- What unfinished tasks are currently "open tabs" in my mind?
- When was the last time I truly felt a sense of completion—what made it possible?
- Do I tend to move my own finish line, like Maria, and if so, why?
- How do unfinished tasks affect my ability to rest, sleep, or be present with others?
- What would it look like to give myself permission to say, "This is enough for today"?

PART III

PRACTISING COGNITIVE CAPACITY

CHAPTER 8

MAKE IT MEANINGFUL

Life is never made unbearable by circumstances, but only by lack of meaning and purpose.

—Viktor Frankl

As we now move into the intersections of the model, we shift from understanding its core parts to exploring how they work together in practice. These intersections are not theoretical niceties; they are the places where intention becomes application, where the framework starts to shape the way you live and work each day. The nuance matters here. It is at the intersections that you find leverage for making better choices, building sustainable habits, and protecting your cognitive capacity in real time.

The first of these intersections is Meaningful, which sits between Criteria and Closure. At its core, creating meaning in our work is not about doing more—it's about making better decisions. Decisions are the invisible thread that ties the start to the finish, linking Criteria (what matters) to Closure (how we finish). Without clear decisions, criteria stay abstract and closure never happens. Meaning is made not just in what you choose to take on, but in the way you carry it through to an end.

Meaningful work is chosen with intention and closed with clarity. When you operate this way, each task leaves behind not just a ticked box but a residue of value: learning gained, alignment reinforced, contribution recognised. Work feels significant, not because it was big or dramatic, but because it was anchored in what mattered and completed in a way that allowed the brain to register its impact.

On a psychological level, meaning aligns us with our values and objectives. We feel that what we do matters, that it contributes, that it adds to something larger than ourselves. On a cognitive level, meaning provides clarity and reduces regret. A finished task that mattered does not weigh on the mind; it frees it. When criteria and closure work in tandem, we are left not with mental residue, but with mental space.

Meaningful work, then, is not accidental. It is engineered—by choosing wisely, finishing deliberately, and refusing to let noise crowd out significance. This is the foundation of resilience and fulfilment in a world that constantly threatens to scatter our attention.

The intersection of meaning gives you the opportunity to move up from busy work (referring back to the model in Chapter 3). The difference between busywork and meaningful work is not always visible from the outside—both involve effort, both fill the calendar, both keep you "working". But the inner experience could not be more different. Busywork is driven by urgency rather than intention. It pulls you into reactive loops that feel draining, repetitive, and often forgettable. Many of these tasks never reach completion or, if they do, they close without reflection, leaving no sense of progress behind.

Meaningful Work vs Busywork

Every professional knows the hollow feeling of a busy day that adds up to very little. You crossed off tasks, answered emails, maybe even attended ten meetings, but at the end, you're left with the nagging question: What did this actually achieve? That's the trap of busywork. It fills time without shaping progress.

Meaningful work feels different. It has a sense of weight, a direction. It connects to something beyond the task itself—an outcome, a value, a purpose. The irony is that meaningful work often doesn't look as "productive" in the moment. It can involve thinking, talking, drafting, or reflecting—things that don't generate instant metrics. But over time, meaningful work compounds while busywork dissolves.

Research backs this up. Organisational psychologist Adam Grant has shown that employees who can see the end-user impact of their work (for instance, scholarship fundraisers who meet the students they support) dramatically increase their output. The tasks didn't change. What changed was their perception of meaning. Purpose fuels persistence.

Meaningful work, by contrast, is driven by intention. It begins with clear criteria, is carried through to closure, and ends with a residue of value—insight gained, alignment clarified, contribution felt. Where busywork consumes your capacity, meaningful work restores it. This is the crucial distinction: one depletes attention and energy without lasting return, while the other clarifies, completes, and strengthens your ability to keep going.

BUSY WORK	MEANINGFUL WORK
Driven by urgency	Driven by intention
Feels draining or forgettable	Feels satisfying or clarifying
Often undone or abandoned	Often completed or reflected on
Closes without reflection	Ends with sense-making or insight
Consumes your capacity	Provides capacity

Become Intentional

The happiness of your life depends upon the quality of your thoughts.

—MARCUS AURELIUS

Every choice signals what you value most in that moment—speed over perfection, long-term gain over short-term comfort, clarity over ambiguity. Decisions aren't just logistical. They are declarations of meaning. When you choose, you implicitly say: "This matters more than that". Even saying, "I'll respond to emails before working on the strategy plan" is a decision that shapes meaning, whether you acknowledge it or not. Decisions define the "why" behind our actions. Our decisions carve meaning into otherwise neutral tasks.

Wes Adams and Tamara Myles, in their book *Meaningful Work*, argue that meaning isn't confined to "creative" or high-prestige roles. Through years of applied research across industries, they found that when people feel their work matters, they are more inspired, more loyal, and more productive—even in sectors that are often overlooked, such as data centers, call centers, or beauty salons. Their findings disrupt the myth that only certain jobs can be meaningful. Instead, meaning is less about the nature of the work and more about how it is framed, led, and experienced.

What stands out in their research is how small gestures by leaders ripple into disproportionate effects. It doesn't always take a grand mission statement or a sweeping corporate rebrand to create meaning. Sometimes it's as simple as a shared tea break at the same time every day, which becomes a ritual of connection. In these moments, colleagues step away from transactional roles and remember they're part of a team, part of something bigger.

From a leadership perspective, this insight is gold. Leaders often assume that cultivating meaning requires expensive perks or radical redesigns of jobs. Yet Adams and Myles show that it's the micro-rituals and deliberate acknowledgements of humanity that most reliably anchor people to their work. A short conversation about why a task matters, a moment of recognition, or a pause for shared connection can transform a routine job into a role with resonance.

This is a reminder that meaning doesn't trickle down from lofty vision statements alone. It is co-created daily, often in the margins of the workday. Leaders who understand this shift their focus from telling people what the company stands for, to designing small, recurring experiences where people can feel it.

Making a decision is also an act of accountability. As long as we linger in options, we can avoid responsibility. But deciding forces us to own a direction.

Making a decision is also an act of accountability. As long as we linger in options, we can avoid responsibility. But deciding forces us to own a direction. In this sense, decisions don't just create meaning in tasks; they create meaning in identity. William James, often called the father of psychology, wrote: "When you have to make a choice and don't make it, that is in itself a choice". Refusing to decide is a decision too—one that leaves meaning up to others, or to chaos.

How to enhance your decision-making in a way that supports your cognitive capacity? Here are six strategies for you to implement:

- Bias awareness
- Design decision premises
- Satisfice
- Remove ambiguity
- Capture decisions
- Strategic underperformance

Bias Awareness

In Chapter 5, when we covered Criteria, the concept of biases and how they create our perception of the world was discussed. As we're looking for strategies to enhance our decision-making and make our work meaningful, we need to dive deeper into biases as they are the invisible lenses that colour every decision.

Psychologists have catalogued dozens, and here are some to bring your awareness to:

- **Confirmation bias**—favouring information that supports what you already believe, e.g., overlooking data that is not in line with your opinion.
- **Availability heuristic**—judging based on what's easiest to recall, not what's most accurate, e.g., believing you need a security system installed because you hear about a local event on the news.
- **Salience bias**—overweighting or overvaluing surprising or prominent information, e.g., fearing plane crashes more than car crashes.
- **Ostrich effect**—avoiding information you fear might be unpleasant or threatening, ignoring bad news, e.g., avoiding bills or medical checkups.
- **Planning fallacy**—underestimating how long things will take, e.g., making your to-do list for the day unachievable long.

The last one is important to discuss further. The planning fallacy leads to overcommitment, stress, and inefficiency. When we underestimate time, we crowd our calendars, stretch our capacity, and end up behind—which fuels frustration and burnout. This chronic underestimating is because we base our decisions on best-case scenarios. It's not a time management issue—it's a cognitive capacity challenge. Catch yourself on this one!

These biases aren't flaws; they're shortcuts. They help the brain move quickly in a noisy world. But left unchecked, they distort meaning. Kahneman's *Thinking, Fast and Slow* tells us that our "System

1" thinking—the quick, intuitive mode—is powerful but prone to bias. "System 2"—the slower, deliberate mode—catches errors but tires easily. Meaningful decision-making requires knowing when to slow down and check the lens.

Awareness of bias doesn't mean eliminating it—that's impossible. What it does mean is creating the space to pause, question, and correct for distortions before they shape your choices. When you recognise that your brain will default to shortcuts, you can deliberately slow down, test assumptions, and weigh alternatives with greater clarity. This is the link between criteria and closure: meaningful decisions are not the absence of bias, but the result of noticing it and then choosing with intention. In practice, bias awareness is less about perfect rationality and more about reclaiming agency—so your decisions reflect what truly matters, not just what your brain finds easiest or most familiar.

Design Decision Premises

We make thousands of decisions daily—and most of them are biased, rushed, and poorly framed. But when we design the conditions in which decisions are made—the premises—we regain clarity and control. A well-designed decision starts before the decision itself. It begins with reducing cognitive load and building the mental environment to filter, focus, and follow through. This is about setting up your brain to succeed, not just trying harder in the moment.

Annie Duke makes a crucial point in *How to Decide*: most of the work of decision-making happens before the decision. If you set poor premises, even a logical process will yield poor outcomes.

Garbage in, garbage out. One of Duke's strongest insights is the idea of separating the quality of a decision from its outcome. You can make a high-quality decision and still get a poor outcome if chance intervenes, just as you can make a poor decision and get lucky. The danger in overloaded workplaces is that we judge our decisions only by results, not by process. That erodes confidence and fuels regret. By focusing on premises—structuring information, clarifying values, reducing noise—we not only improve decision quality but also reclaim peace of mind when outcomes don't go our way.

This is where meaningful enters the frame. Premises are the rules, values, or criteria you use to judge options. If those are vague, reactive, or borrowed from others, your decisions wobble. If they are intentional and meaningful, your choices align with who you are and what matters most. So clear criteria are essential, but premises add the detail.

Premises also simplify. When you know in advance what matters, you don't agonise over every option. You filter. It's like setting a compass bearing before a hike: once chosen, every step is easier. Without it, you wander, second-guessing at every fork.

Picture yourself in front of the TV at 8pm, exhausted, remote in hand. Hundreds of channels, endless scrolling, and before you know it, you've settled—again—for something average. Now imagine you had a simple, prefiltered list: "Shows I watch when I want comfort. Shows when I want to learn. Shows when I want lightness". Suddenly, the choice becomes easier—and more satisfying. The same principle applies beyond the TV screen. We can prefilter our work tasks, client emails, meeting invitations, and even daily priorities. When the criteria are set in advance, the moment of decision is no longer a struggle; it becomes an act of alignment.

Personally, I only watch series these days, and my rule is this: on the website IMDB, a show has to score at least 8 out of 10, unless it comes highly recommended by a friend. It may sound small, but that filter saves me time, avoids disappointment, and ensures my attention goes where it's worthwhile.

Designing premises creates your boundaries and non-negotiables. They are your preset options for what you can anticipate in your preparation for when you have less capacity to make decisions. Without them, decision-making collapses under noise. With them, you've just saved yourself some mental bandwidth and a better result.

Satisfice

Herbert Simon, Nobel Prize–winning economist and psychologist, coined the term satisficing to describe how humans actually make decisions in the real world. The word "satisfice" is a blend of satisfy and suffice. So, to satisfice means: to accept a solution that is satisfactory and sufficient, rather than the absolute best; and to balance limited time, energy, and information against the need to make progress.

Faced with overwhelming complexity, we rarely search for the absolute best option—what Simon called "maximising". Instead, we look for an option that is good enough to meet our criteria, and then we stop. This isn't laziness; it's survival. With limited time, attention, and cognitive capacity, satisficing protects us from paralysis by analysis. In practice, it means defining your standards up front—what "good enough" looks like—and moving forward once those are met.

In a world of infinite information, optimisation is an illusion. You can't try every restaurant before choosing dinner, or test every career path before accepting a job. Chasing the "perfect" choice leads to paralysis and regret. Barry Schwartz's research on the paradox of choice shows that maximisers—those who seek the best possible option—tend to be less happy, less satisfied, and more anxious. Satisficers, in contrast, move faster and feel more content.

Satisficing gives us clarity. When you know what is meaningful, you can set a threshold: if the option meets these key criteria (and check your decision premises too), it's enough. That frees you from endless comparison. It also frees you from guilt. Choosing "good enough" on the less meaningful decisions preserves energy for the choices that truly matter.

Think of it as triage. Not every decision deserves the same attention. The colour of your office chair? Satisfice. The strategic direction of your company? Deliberate. By consciously satisficing on the small stuff, you protect your bandwidth for the big stuff.

Remove Ambiguity

Ambiguity drains meaning. It is one of the ten saboteurs to cognitive capacity we discussed in Chapter 3. When expectations are vague, roles unclear, or criteria hidden, people spin in circles. They pour energy into guessing what matters instead of doing what matters. The result is frustration, disengagement, and wasted effort.

Psychologists have shown that ambiguity is a major driver of workplace stress. One Gallup study found that only half of employees strongly agree they know what is expected of them at work. The rest operate in a fog. Without clarity, even hardworking teams flounder.

Meaning thrives on specificity. Clear criteria reduce noise. Brené Brown puts it bluntly: "Clear is kind. Unclear is unkind". Vagueness may feel polite or flexible, but it robs people of direction. Leaders who clearly state what is expected—and what isn't—unlock meaning for their teams.

Removing ambiguity requires courage. It means saying no to vague projects, asking clarifying questions, and pushing back when goals are fuzzy. It means designing work with sharper edges. The reward is energy freed from second-guessing and redirected into action that matters. It protects your cognitive capacity.

Capture Decisions

Meaningful work doesn't depend only on good decisions in the moment. It also depends on capturing those decisions so they don't unravel or get forgotten. Psychologists Sendhil Mullainathan and Eldar Shafir, in their book *Scarcity*, show that cognitive bandwidth shrinks when we operate under pressure. When bandwidth is tight, even simple decisions slip. We forget commitments, overlook details, or duplicate effort.

The solution is simply: externalise decisions. Capture them. Write them down. Record the rationale. Store them in a trusted system. David Allen's *Getting Things Done* popularised this approach: capture every decision or commitment so the brain doesn't have to hold it. And we now know your brain is already overloaded, so it's kind, clear and essential to externalise. Your team will thank you.

Why does this matter for meaning? Because unrecorded decisions decay. A team may spend hours debating strategy, but if the outcome isn't captured, ambiguity creeps back. Individuals may make commitments in meetings, but if they're not written down, they vanish under the flood of inputs. Without capture, decisions dissolve—and meaning with them.

Capturing decisions is not bureaucracy. It is protection. It ensures that the energy spent on making meaningful decisions isn't wasted. In this sense, writing things down is an act of respect—for your future self, and for those who rely on you.

Strategic Underperformance

We can't do everything well. Trying to excel at everything dilutes meaning. Frances Frei and Anne Morriss, in their work on leadership, argue that great organisations deliberately underperform in some areas to excel in others. They choose trade-offs.This is the essence of strategic underperformance. It's not neglect; it's focus. Strategic underperformance means accepting that some tasks will get only minimal energy. Not every email requires a crafted reply. Not every project deserves innovation. By underperforming strategically, you avoid spreading yourself so thin that nothing is meaningful.

This requires courage because culture pressures us to maximise in every direction. But meaning demands trade-offs. If everything matters equally, nothing truly matters. Choosing where not to excel is the hidden half of choosing where to excel.

In Closing

Meaning is not found in sheer effort or in the number of items ticked off a list. It emerges in the space between Criteria and Closure—when what you take on is aligned with what matters, and when you carry it through to a clear end. Every decision you make is a small act of meaning-making. When you choose intentionally, follow through deliberately, and release the work with clarity, you are not just completing tasks—you are shaping the story of your contribution.

The trap of busywork will always be there: endless emails, reactive loops, the churn of activity that consumes but never restores capacity. The opportunity, however, lies in the opposite direction. Meaningful work compounds. It creates alignment, fuels resilience, and leaves you lighter rather than heavier. The research is clear, but so is the lived experience: the days that stand out are not the days you did the most, but the days you did what mattered.

As you move forward, remember that choosing is an act of intention. Closing is an act of release. Together, they free your capacity, sharpen your focus, and allow your work to contribute to something larger than the immediate moment. It will transition you from busy work to meaningful work.

The next intersection we'll explore— Methodical—will show how Criteria and Chunking combine to give structure to that intention. If Meaningful is about choosing and closing with clarity, Methodical is about building the systems that make such clarity sustainable.

Action Steps:

1. **Create your own action plan** to enhance your skills in the six strategies:
   - Bias awareness
   - Design decision premises
   - Satisfice
   - Remove ambiguity
   - Capture decisions
   - Strategic underperformance

2. **Have your own criteria** for what growth or success in this would look like.

3. **Try it out** and set a calendar appointment to review this.

4. **Try two strategies** in the same manner with your team.

Ask Yourself:

- When was the last time I ended a day feeling truly meaningful rather than merely busy? What was different?

- Which choices in my work life do I feel paralysed by too many options?

- How much of my stress comes not from workload, but from ambiguity? Where could clarity restore meaning?

- Where in my life could satisficing free energy for what really matters?

- Where might I deliberately choose to underperform so I can truly excel elsewhere?

CHAPTER 9

MAKE IT METHODICAL

Chaos is merely order waiting to be deciphered.

—JOSÉ SARAMAGO

The second intersection is Methodical, which sits between Criteria and Chunking. Making your workflow methodical is not about rigid structure but having supportive systems in place that, rather than overwhelm you, support you in your productivity. Methodical, linking Criteria (what matters) to Chunking (how we process) makes it practical. Methodical is the tangible scaffold in how you go about your work every day. Where Meaningful helped us choose better, Methodical is to create structure—about building an intentional workflow that protects cognitive capacity.

Our pathway to productivity is rarely a straight line. Work comes at us in unpredictable ways—shifting priorities, incoming requests, and unexpected interruptions. Without a method, we fall into frantic work mode: chasing the loudest task, juggling inputs, and losing track of priorities. A methodical approach creates anchors. It ensures that instead of being pulled into every current, we navigate toward where we want to go.

But what can we do to stay on top of things and to stay on track?

Consider project teams that manage tasks through scattered email threads and sticky notes. They spend more time searching for updates than making progress. Compare this with teams using a clear task system: roles defined, inputs sorted, next steps visible. The difference isn't talent or effort—it's method.

Methodical Work vs Frantic Work

Most of us begin with the best intentions. We want to work on what matters, guided by our criteria. Yet the reality of modern work rarely looks intentional. It looks messy—an overflowing inbox, half-written notes, a dozen tabs open, three meetings running into each other. Chaos is the norm.

The problem isn't that we lack effort. Busy professionals work harder than ever, but without method, effort disperses like spilled water. Chaos absorbs energy without giving clarity in return. To reclaim it, we must be methodical. Being methodical doesn't mean rigid or bureaucratic. It means having a repeatable way to handle the flood of inputs and decisions. Method gives criteria a channel and gives chunks a process. Without it, we fall prey to randomness— reacting to whatever shouts loudest instead of shaping our own priorities.

FRANTIC WORK	METHODICAL WORK
Driven by reaction	Driven by process
Feels scattered or overwhelming	Feels structured and clear
Tasks get lost or duplicated	Tasks move forward with visibility
Constant switching drains focus	Workflow reduces friction and protects focus

How to Not Forget Things

Psychologists tell us that working memory is brutally limited. George Miller's famous "magic number" suggested we can hold only seven (plus or minus two) chunks of information at a time. More recent research lowers that number to four. Yet on any given day, most professionals juggle dozens of commitments, deadlines, and names.

Without a method, forgetting is inevitable. You promise to follow up, but the thought vanishes in the crush of emails. You start a report, but it's lost under new requests. The brain wasn't built to be a filing cabinet.

David Allen's *Getting Things Done* popularised this truth: "Your mind is for having ideas, not holding them". He describes unclosed commitments as "open loops"—any unfinished obligation, whether it's returning a phone call, submitting a report, or even buying milk on the way home. The brain doesn't distinguish between a million-dollar project and a trivial errand. Both occupy mental space; both remain alive in the background until resolved or captured.

The problem is that our brains are poor storage systems. They don't have an indexed filing drawer; they have a sticky whiteboard where everything smears together. Neuroscience backs this up. Recall the Zeigarnik effect we discussed earlier? It refers to the fact that people remember unfinished tasks far better than completed ones. Your brain holds on to the open loop, nudging you with a sense of incompletion, even if you can't articulate what's missing.

This explains why stress often lingers without a clear cause. You may feel tense during your commute home, not because you consciously remember what you left undone, but because your brain does. Open loops hum quietly in the background, consuming bandwidth.

David Allen's brilliance was not in inventing a new insight, but in operationalising it. His system of external capture—writing everything down into a trusted system—turns the sticky whiteboard into a clear canvas. By moving commitments out of the head and into reliable containers, the brain is released from its endless Post-it-note shuffle.

Think of your mind as a computer. When you try to use it as a hard drive, it slows down. Background processes multiply, memory fragments, and performance drops. But when you offload the files to external storage—whether that's a notebook, an app, or even a whiteboard—the processor is freed to do what it does best: solve problems, create, and imagine.

The stress of forgetting, then, is not limited to the mistake of a missed deadline. It is the constant low-grade anxiety of sensing something unresolved. It's like carrying a backpack with unknown contents—too heavy to ignore, but too vague to unload. Only by capturing the commitments in a trusted system can you take the weight off your shoulders.

Methodical work builds trust in yourself. By designing a reliable intake layer—a place where every input, idea, or task is caught—you reduce the anxiety of forgetting. Like a net under a tightrope walker, the intake doesn't stop you from falling, but it ensures you don't crash.

How to build your trustworthy system in a way that supports your cognitive capacity? Here are two strategies for you to implement:

- Task management—staying on top
- Input management—staying on track

Task Management—Staying on Top

A client once told me she woke up at 2am, panicked about a meeting she hadn't prepared for. The funny thing was—the meeting wasn't even until the following week. But because her tasks lived across emails, scraps of paper, and her head, she didn't trust her system. That mistrust meant her brain kept rehearsing and reminding her at the worst possible times. Once she implemented a simple capture-and-review system, she could finally sleep through the night knowing nothing important would slip.

Even with a strong intake system, the sheer volume of tasks can swamp us. Overwhelm is not just about forgetting; it's about facing too many remembered tasks at once. The list itself becomes oppressive.

Here, methodical work means chunking tasks into meaningful groups and then applying criteria to decide which groups to tackle. Cognitive load theory explains why this matters: the brain processes grouped information more efficiently than scattered fragments. A to-do list of twenty unlinked items feels impossible. The same list, organised into three categories—clients, strategy, and admin—suddenly feels workable.

Yet grouping alone is not enough. The key is to decide which chunks align with meaning. This is where criteria and chunking converge through method. Without method, you either overcommit or stall. With it, you can look at the categories and say: Today belongs to strategy. Admin waits.

Alex Pang, in his book *Rest*, emphasises that capacity isn't built by doing everything but by knowing what to leave undone. A method allows you to shelve tasks without guilt. They're not forgotten; they're parked in a trusted system, ready for when the time is right. This is how you stay on top of things.

Input Management—Staying on Track

One of the greatest threats to methodical work is uncontrolled input. The modern worker faces hundreds of emails, chat messages, notifications, and documents daily. Without a system, these inputs collide and accumulate until focus collapses.

A method allows you to
shelve tasks without guilt.
They're not forgotten;
they're parked in a trusted
system, ready for when
the time is right.

Cal Newport calls this the hyperactive hive mind—the unstructured flow of messages and tasks that traps organisations in a state of permanent reaction. In this environment, meaningful work struggles to survive because attention is constantly diverted to whatever arrives next.

Method provides the antidote: an intake layer that catches inputs without letting them dictate your actions. This is not about responding instantly to every message, but about having a predictable path: all emails get processed at a set time, meeting notes land in one system, and ideas get captured in a single notebook. The point is not speed, but trust. You trust that no input is lost, so you don't have to chase every ping.

Gloria Mark's continued research on interruptions found that after interruptions (external or self-chosen), people often had to consult multiple information sources again (emails, notes, shared systems) to reconstruct where they were. Mark observed that people who had structured systems for where incoming information went (for example, always logging tasks in a single project management tool, or filing emails consistently) resumed work faster and with less stress. Those who kept inputs scattered (sticky notes, inbox, chat windows, memory) were far more fragmented and reported higher time pressure.

If you decide immediately where an input belongs (calendar, task list, project board, info storage), you prevent the resumption cost of later hunting through scattered places. Gloria Mark's data shows that interruptions are inevitable, but the cost multiplies when there is no clear "home" for inputs. By having one system, you're not eliminating interruptions, but you're eliminating the chaos that comes when your brain or desk becomes the storage unit.

The cost of unmanaged input is not just wasted time but fractured cognition. A method that filters input—deciding what to capture, when to process, and what to ignore—is therefore not optional. It is the foundation of preserving capacity.

Methodical Work in Practice

What does methodical work look like day-to-day?

A single intake system for tasks and ideas, so nothing is scattered.

A rhythm for processing inputs—emails at 10am and 3pm, not constantly.

Chunked categories of tasks or projects, reviewed against clear criteria.

Strategic deferrals, where non-urgent tasks are deliberately parked.

In Closing

When Anne, a senior project manager in a global engineering firm, first came to one of my workshops, she was exhausted. Her days blurred into a storm of emails, shifting priorities, and last-minute crises. She prided herself on being responsive, but behind the scenes, she was running on fumes. "It feels like my brain is a browser with fifty tabs open," she told me.

We started with something simple: building a method to capture everything, process inputs at set times, and chunk tasks into meaningful groups. Within weeks, her stress shifted. She still had the same workload, but she described a profound difference:

"For the first time in years, I feel like I can actually think again".

That's the essence of methodical work. It doesn't eliminate pressure or remove demands. It frees cognitive capacity that was previously hijacked by forgotten commitments, scattered inputs, and endless mental juggling. By offloading the noise into a trusted system, the brain regains its natural strengths: problem-solving, creativity, and strategic thinking.

Cognitive capacity is not about working harder. It is about protecting the mental bandwidth to work with clarity. Method is the quiet structure that creates that protection. Just as traffic signals don't reduce the number of cars but prevent collisions, method doesn't make the world less complex—it makes it navigable.

And here's the deeper truth: methodical work is not about being tidy for tidiness' sake. It's about ensuring that when the truly meaningful work arrives—the strategic insight, the crucial decision, the human conversation—you have the capacity to show up fully. Without method, you drown in noise. With it, you create the mental space where meaning can take root.

Meaningful productivity is not about squeezing in more, but about moving with less friction. Method is the invisible scaffolding that allows criteria to shape action and chunking to simplify complexity. Without method, both collapse. With it, the pieces align into flow.

Action Steps:

1. **Create your own method** or review your task management and input management process to ensure it captures your tasks and ideas.
2. **Assess** whether you act on this method consistently.
3. In the same manner, **implement a capture method** with your team.

Ask Yourself:

- How much do I rely on memory during my workday?
- When does my workday feel most chaotic? What's missing from my method in those moments?
- How many interruptions do I face in a typical hour?
- What's my intake system for new inputs? Is it predictable—or ad hoc?
- What tasks could I strategically defer, without guilt, to preserve capacity?

CHAPTER 10

MAKE IT MANAGEABLE

Success always demands a greater effort.

—WINSTON CHURCHILL

Churchill spoke those words in the context of war, but for today's professionals, the battlefield looks different. Instead of artillery fire, it's the ping of notifications. Instead of bombs, it's calendar alerts detonating across your day. And instead of enemies charging the front, it's the endless flow of emails, messages, and requests rushing from every direction.

The final intersection is Manageable, which sits between Chunking and Closure. This is about providing you with the right tools and strategies for it to be cognitively sustainable. Manageable, linking Chunking (how we process) and Closure (how we finish) is not about technical applications or productivity hacks, but knowing what your brain needs to deal with interruptions, distractions, and new input.

Where Meaningful helped us choose better, Methodical created structure, and Manageable will help us to keep it together to maintain our cognitive capacity.

We often think success means pushing harder. Stay later. Answer faster. Carry more. Yet the paradox of modern work is that more effort often makes things worse. The harder we try to absorb everything, the more fragmented our focus becomes. We confuse stamina with capacity, forgetting that the brain is not a muscle that strengthens with strain, but a battery that drains faster under chaotic load.

Gloria Mark at UC Irvine has spent two decades studying interruptions in the workplace. Her findings are sobering. The average knowledge worker switches screens or tasks every forty seconds. Once interrupted, it takes over twenty-three minutes to return to the original task—if you return at all. Many never do. In the meantime, stress rises, error rates increase, and the quality of thought erodes.

Consider a typical morning. You open your laptop with the intention of finishing a report. Within minutes, a chat notification pulls you into a colleague's question. While answering, you see an email subject line flash across your inbox—an urgent client issue. You click it. Then your phone buzzes with a text. By the time you return to the report, you've forgotten the thread of reasoning that was fresh ten minutes ago. You reread, but it feels heavy. You push harder, but progress stalls. The day dissolves into fragments, and by evening, you are exhausted but unsatisfied. This is the reality of unmanaged cognition. Disruption is no longer the exception. It is the operating system. Without ballast, the boat tips at every gust of wind. Without method, every ping carries you off course.

To make work manageable, we need systems that protect cognition against this storm. Not by removing all wind—it's impossible to eliminate interruptions entirely—but by building stability into how we sail. Manageable work is not about perfection or control. It is about creating conditions where effort is sustainable.

Manageable Work vs Hard Work

Many professionals know the temptation of slipping into "hard work" mode—head down, grinding through the to-do list, fuelled by grit alone. On the surface, it looks admirable: long hours, constant effort, never letting up. But inside, it feels different. Hard work is effort-heavy and energy-draining. It runs on adrenaline and willpower, not on structure or strategy. You finish the day exhausted, yet unsure if your effort truly moved the needle.

Manageable work, by contrast, feels steady and sustainable. It isn't about avoiding effort—it's about working in a way that protects capacity rather than burns it. Manageable work anticipates disruptions instead of being constantly blindsided by them. It builds rituals and routines that act as scaffolding, so memory alone doesn't carry the load. It honours clear priorities and boundaries, so not everything feels urgent. The result is that you end the day with energy preserved, not depleted.

When we overload working memory with too many competing demands, performance collapses. Manageable systems—rituals, routines, boundaries—reduce that load. Instead of firefighting, you're focusing. Instead of running on fumes, you're conserving for what matters.

This distinction matters because hard work is seductive. It looks productive in the moment, but is unsustainable in the long run. Manageable work may look quieter, but it's what allows you to show up consistently, make sound decisions, and preserve clarity. In other words—hard work spends capacity; manageable work protects it.

HARD WORK	**MANAGEABLE WORK**
Constantly disruptive, reactive	Anticipates disruptions
Feels draining and scattered	Feels steady and sustainable
Relies on memory alone	Uses rituals and routines
Works extra hours	Clear priorities & boundaries
Ends in fatigue	Ends with energy preserved

How to make the way you work manageable that supports your cognitive capacity? Here are three strategies for you to implement:

- Cognitive nets
- Cognitive recovery
- Care less

Cognitive Nets

The Apollo 11 mission was one of the most complex human endeavours ever attempted. Astronauts had to operate under extraordinary cognitive demands: every move mattered, errors could be fatal, and communication delays left little room for indecision.

How did they manage it? They didn't rely on sheer memory or willpower. They relied on checklists.

One of the best ways to stabilise cognition is to create cognitive nets—external supports that catch the things our minds inevitably drop.

Checklists are one form of what Atul Gawande, in *The Checklist Manifesto*, calls cognitive nets—structures that catch human fallibility. Apollo astronauts used them for everything from engine burns to donning suits. Surgeons use them before operations. Pilots use them before every flight. These nets don't add intelligence; they reduce error. They catch what the brain drops.

Cognitive psychologists Altmann and Trafton studied what happens when people are interrupted mid-task. Their research shows that unless we mark exactly where we left off, memory of that state decays rapidly. Imagine leaving halfway through a recipe, then returning later. Did you already add the salt? Did you set the timer? Without a marker, you're left to guess. A checklist, or even a scribbled "last step done", prevents wasted effort and mistakes.

Why do these nets matter so much? Because modern work is not a straight line; it is an obstacle course of interruptions. Each time you stop and restart, you lose momentum. Nets reduce the cost of resumption. They let you pick up the thread quickly, without reconstructing the entire context from scratch. Our cognitive nets— whether a sticky note, a digital board, or a ritualised team process— catch the details that our brains are bound to drop.

And they scale. A solo entrepreneur can use a daily notebook to net their ideas. A large organisation can use structured project boards. A family can use a shared calendar on the fridge. The form is flexible, but the principle is universal: do not trust memory to hold what a system can catch. A single sticky note on your desk is useful, but fragile.

So the challenge is not whether you're smart enough or disciplined enough to keep up. The key is to reframe productivity. Instead of asking, "How do I get better at remembering?" the question becomes, "How do I ensure I don't have to remember at all?"

Other research deepens the point. Psychologists Evan Risko and Sam Gilbert coined the term cognitive offloading to describe how humans routinely push mental tasks into the environment. We use notes, calendars, apps, bookmarks, alarms, and even the simple habit of putting our keys in the same bowl by the door. These behaviours are not signs of forgetfulness, but of efficiency. Offloading reduces the burden on working memory, which is notoriously limited—able to hold just a handful of items at once. By externalising, we free up scarce mental slots for higher-level problem solving.

Gilles Einstein and Mark McDaniel built on this with experiments on intention memory—our ability to remember to act in the future. Participants who wrote down their intentions or set external cues were far more likely to follow through than those who tried to "just remember". The brain, it turns out, is brilliant at generating ideas but poor at storing them. Like trying to hold water in your hands, the details inevitably leak. Writing things down or embedding cues in the environment provides the container. They demonstrated that people recall more accurately when they externalise intentions rather than trust memory.

Cognitive anthropologist Edwin Hutchins extended this insight by observing airline crews. In a cockpit, no single pilot carries all the cognitive load. Instead, thinking is distributed across people and artifacts: flight charts, instrument panels, spoken callouts, and procedural checklists. When the co-pilot reads out altitude, when the captain confirms speed, when a checklist verifies flap settings, each moment is a node in a web of nets. Safety depends not on flawless memory, but on the reliability of distributed cognition.

The implications are profound. It means that productivity is not simply a matter of individual grit, but of designing environments that support cognition. A doctor double-checking a patient chart, a lawyer highlighting a case precedent, a parent setting a timer to remember the oven—all are practising cognitive offloading. In each case, the external tool acts as a net, catching what the mind would otherwise drop.

The metaphor is simple: fishing nets catch what would otherwise slip through the water. Cognitive nets catch what would otherwise slip through attention. They are scaffolding for focus in an environment built for distraction.

Far from being a weakness, offloading is one of humanity's greatest strengths. It is the reason we keep journals, build libraries, use navigation systems, and create shared rituals. These tools are extensions of the mind, multiplying capacity by letting the brain specialise in what it does best: generating insights, making connections, and solving problems. Wherever nets exist, cognition stabilises. Wherever they don't, it frays.

Cognitive Recovery

Even with nets in place, cognitive effort depletes. The question becomes: How do we restore it? Athletes know recovery is part of training. Muscles don't grow stronger in the gym; they grow during rest. The same applies to cognition.

Research on attention residue by Sophie Leroy (which we already covered in Chapter 7, Closure) shows that when you switch tasks without closure, fragments of the previous task linger in the mind. This residue reduces effectiveness on the new task, like trying to sprint while still catching your breath from the last race. Cognitive recovery requires creating rituals that clear residue and reset the system.

These resets don't need to be grand. Sonnentag and Fritz, in their studies on recovery from work stress, identify four essential experiences: detachment (psychological distance from work), relaxation, mastery (engaging in something new), and control (choosing how to spend your time). A ten-minute walk without your phone can provide detachment. Cooking a new recipe can provide mastery. The point is not the activity itself but the way it allows the mind to unclench.

Micro-resets matter too. Breathing exercises, brief stretches, stepping away from the desk to refill a glass of water—all serve as small closures that prevent attention from fraying entirely. The list is endless; apparently, doodling helps, yoga nidra is amazing, brain wave sounds support you, and the practice of doing nothing is beneficial. Try what suits you. Without recovery, effort piles into exhaustion. With it, effort is renewed. You need it!

Cognitive nets catch what would otherwise slip through attention. They are scaffolding for focus in an environment built for distraction.

Care Less

It sounds counterintuitive, even irresponsible. But sometimes the most sustainable way to preserve cognition is to care less. Not about everything—just about the things that don't matter. It protects your own personal boundaries by not caring so much about your work. You don't need to ruminate over the actions of this one colleague for the entire week, or stress about how the other department will go through their restructure. Of course, you care, but perhaps just not as much.

Celeste Headlee, in her book *Do Nothing*, warns against the culture of constant striving, where even leisure becomes performance. The paradox is that by trying to care equally about everything, we dilute our ability to care deeply about anything. Lao Tzu put it centuries earlier: "By letting go, it all gets done."

Caring less isn't disengagement. It's discernment. It means deciding not to spend mental bandwidth on every ping, every headline, every fleeting demand. It is saying: this matters, that doesn't. Without this filter, capacity drains into trivia. With it, capacity stays for what is meaningful.

In Closing

If Meaningful sets the compass and Methodical provides the map for the journey, then Manageability is the ballast in the boat. It keeps the journey stable when winds of distraction blow hardest. Without it, even the best direction and organisation collapse under pressure.

Cognitive nets, recovery rituals, and the discipline of caring less are not indulgences; they are lifelines. They transform work from a storm of interruptions into a voyage you can sustain. The promise of manageability is not easy. The seas remain rough. But with ballast, you sail upright, capable of carrying meaning across the waves rather than being swallowed by them.

Action Steps:

1.   **Try out several cognitive nets:**
     - Checklists.
     - Write it down.
     - State your intent out loud.
2.   **Find out what works for you.**
3.   **Map out your cognitive recovery plan;** create a five-minute version, a thirty-minute version, and a few-hour version.
4.   **Try it out** and set a calendar appointment to review this.
5.   In the same manner, **try two strategies** with your team.

Ask Yourself:

- When do I feel most disrupted in my day?
- What's my current "cognitive net"? Where does it fail to catch things?
- Do I trust my memory too much? What could I offload externally instead?
- What rituals could I implement to help me reset between tasks?
- What's one area of my work where I could consciously care less?

PART IV

MAINTAINING COGNITIVE CAPACITY

CHAPTER 11

THE PRODUCTIVITY CHOICE

Nothing is less productive than to make more efficient what should not be done at all.

—PETER DRUCKER

Most professionals know the Eisenhower Matrix. Urgent vs important. Stephen Covey wrote about it, trainers teach it, managers sketch it on whiteboards. And it works—at least in theory. The trouble is, nobody really has the bandwidth to stop and run every incoming email, meeting request, or task through a matrix before deciding what to do next. In an overloaded world, even the act of prioritising becomes another demand on our cognitive capacity.

That's why I've found it more powerful to stop obsessing over individual tasks and instead pay attention to the mode of work you're in. Think of it less as micromanaging your to-do list and more as zooming out to see the rules under which you're operating. Are you letting urgency rule? Chaos? Sheer activity? Or are you working from clarity and productivity?

The model I use looks like a cousin of the Eisenhower Matrix, but it diagnoses work modes rather than tasks. On the surface, all work looks the same—emails answered, reports written, calls taken. But look deeper, and you'll see that the quality of the mode matters more than the quantity of tasks.

These work modes are also linked to levels 2, 3, 4, and 5 of the model we discussed in Chapter 3. The bottom level, the crisis work mode, and the top level of this work mode model, the capacity work mode, fall outside the scope of this matrix.

- On the left, it indicates your **internal state**; in the top row, you are working focused, and in the bottom row, you are working in a distracted manner.
- At the bottom, it indicates your **external world**; in the left column, you are reactive to input, and in the right column, you are proactive to input.

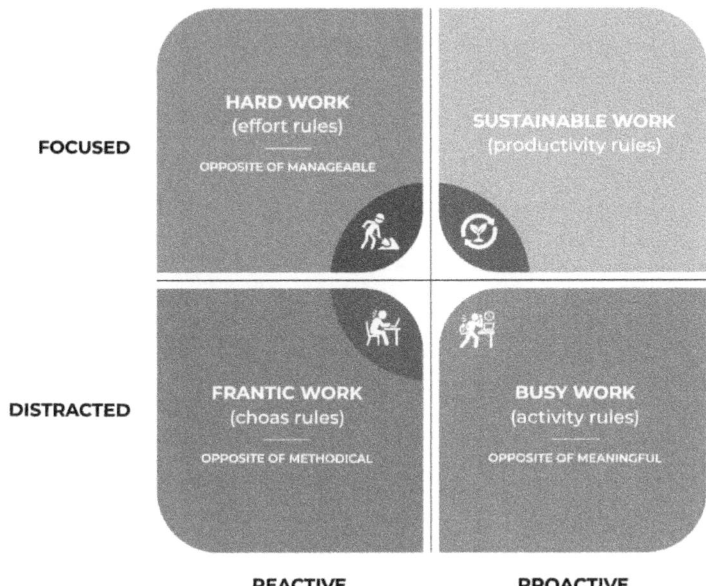

- **Frantic Work** (chaos rules): Reactive, unintentional, scattered. Everything is urgent; nothing is really adding value. This is level 2 of the work mode level.

- **Busy Work** (activity rules): Lots of motion, little progress. You tick boxes but feel hollow at the end of the day. This is level 3 of the work mode level.

- **Hard Work** (effort rules): You're focused but running on grit alone. It's exhausting, not sustainable. This is level 4 of the work mode level.

- **Sustainable Work** (productivity rules): Clarity rules. You're proactive, focused, and your output compounds. This is level 5 of the work mode level.

You won't always be in sustainable work mode. Life and work don't allow it. But awareness is leverage. If you can recognise when you're trapped in frantic, busy, or hard work, you can choose to pivot—even slightly—towards sustainable work.

Because the truth is: sustainable work doesn't happen by accident. It's built on three foundations:

- Work that is meaningful avoids busy work.
- Work that is methodical avoids frantic work.
- Work that is manageable avoids hard work.

You now have the tools and understanding to make that shift.

You have a choice to make.

Not about every single task—none of us has the time for that. But about the mode you operate in.

The real productivity choice, then, is not between one email or another, one meeting or another. It is between modes. Every day, often without noticing, you step into one of these quadrants. You can burn yourself out in frantic work, drift in busy work, or grind through hard work—but none of these will sustain you. The goal is not perfection, but awareness: to catch yourself when you've slipped into chaos, activity, or grit, and to shift deliberately toward sustainable work.

That is where clarity lives, where your energy compounds, and where your contribution feels meaningful. Productivity isn't about squeezing more in; it's about choosing the rules you work under. And the most powerful choice you can make is to work in a way that sustains both your output and yourself.

CHAPTER 12

OFFICE RULES FOR COGNITIVE CAPACITY

Clear is kind. Unclear is unkind.

—BRENÉ BROWN

Most workplaces are full of good people trying to do their best. But the absence of a few simple "rules of the road" means everyone ends up tripping over each other. Messages pile up without context. Meetings sprawl without conclusions. Boundaries are crossed without bad intent, simply because no one named them.

Office rules are not about rigidity or control. They're about respect. They're agreements that protect everyone's cognitive bandwidth, so the office becomes a place where energy is spent on the work itself rather than the friction around it.

In my work with organisations, I've seen the same three areas come up again and again: communication, decisions and meetings, and boundaries. When left unstructured, these elements quietly drain capacity every single day. When they're set up well, they multiply clarity and energy. They support cognitive capacity.

Rule 1: Communication Contracts

Every message is a withdrawal from someone else's cognitive bank. Yet we often send them without thinking about the cost. One workplace I worked with had Slack, Teams, email, WhatsApp, and text messages all in use at once. Some people checked everything; others checked none. Messages were missed, duplicated, or answered three times. The frustration wasn't about bad intentions—it was about a lack of agreements.

A communication contract is simply a shared agreement on how the team uses its tools. It doesn't need to be long or complex. In fact, the shorter, the better. The point is to remove uncertainty so people stop burning energy wondering: "Should I email, or message? Do they expect an answer tonight? Do I have to reply-all?" That way, we are all clear on our communication methods and expectations.

Action Steps:

1. **Map out your communication:**

    - What tools do we use? List everything—email, Teams, WhatsApp, Trello—whatever your team is using.
    - What do we use each tool for? Define what each tool is for (and not for). For example, emails might be for external comms, Teams for quick chats, and Trello for project updates.

- What's the etiquette? Agree on response times. Should emails be answered within an hour or within 24 hours? Where do urgent messages go? What counts as "urgent"?

2. **Email hygiene (sender):**

- Have a clear purpose to send; know what is needed before you communicate.
- Use formatting options (colours, bold, font, tag) to highlight actions. Don't be afraid it's too direct; it makes it clear and easy to process for the receiver.
- Agree on email hashtags within your organisation #needyou #info #decisiontime.
- Give feedback to sender ("I don't need to be included next time" or "I don't understand what you want me to do").

3. **Email hygiene (receiver):**

- Check email at regular times, not all the time.
- Turn off inbox notifications. You don't need to know about the eighty times an email comes in a day.
- Don't make your inbox your to-do list. You'll end up re-reading and cherry-picking; it adds to the chaotic mode of working.
- Read once on every single incoming message and decide what needs to happen (don't go back to it).

4. **Busy buffers (consider trying these out with your team):**

- "No meeting Wednesdays".
- No email Friday mornings.
- Create "office hours" of when you are available.

These rules aren't about controlling people. They're about reducing noise, so meaning can rise to the surface. Communication is currency. When it's spent wisely, capacity is preserved.

Rule 2: Decision & Meeting Hygiene

If communication is the bloodstream of an organisation, decisions are its heartbeat. Yet in many workplaces, decisions are fuzzy, undocumented, or endlessly revisited. Meetings, meanwhile, swell into two-hour marathons where nobody is quite sure what was agreed.

The hidden cost is lost cognitive capacity. Without clear decision hygiene, people carry unresolved questions in their heads. Without meeting hygiene, people lose hours in vague conversations that could have been fifteen minutes.

Action Steps:

1. **Premises first**—before debating, agree on what facts or assumptions are in play. Be clear on your criteria. Most circular discussions are just people operating from different angles.
2. **Reversibility check**—Jeff Bezos popularised this: ask whether the decision is easily reversible. If yes, decide fast. If no, pause longer. Not every decision deserves a committee.
3. **Decision log**—keep a shared record of decisions—who made them, when, and why. This reduces the endless "didn't we already decide this?" conversations.
4. **Meeting hygiene:**
   - Have a clear agenda. If there isn't one, don't meet.

- Set time boundaries. End meetings at 25 or 50 minutes instead of defaulting to the hour. The constraint sharpens focus.

- End with closure. Always end by stating: what was decided, what are the next steps, and who owns them.

Decision and meeting hygiene act like a metronome. They keep the rhythm steady, so energy isn't wasted on confusion.

Rule 3: Boundaries & Capacity Language

Boundaries are not walls. They're gates—clear, visible, and managed with respect. Without boundaries, work seeps into every corner of the day. People answer emails at midnight, agree to unrealistic deadlines, and say yes to every request. Not because they want to, but because they don't feel they can say no. The result is burnout.

The fix is to make boundaries explicit and normalise capacity language.

Action Steps:

1. **Office hours**—a manager sets expectations: "I don't reply to emails after 6pm If something is urgent, text me." This doesn't block emergencies, but it makes the norm clear. Honour these.

2. **Capacity language**—instead of saying "no" (and not supporting the team) or worse, even "yes" (and risk overcommitting), you say, "I can help with this—next Tuesday." Or, "That's important, but it's not possible alongside these other priorities. Which should we drop?"

Or my favourite: "I don't have capacity for that right now." Boundaries become collaborative rather than confrontational.

3. **Escalation etiquette**—teach people what counts as urgent and how to raise it. If everything is urgent, nothing is.

4. **Review & adjust**—if it isn't working, change it.

Boundaries preserve cognitive bandwidth, not by reducing effort, but by focusing it. They are the fence that keeps your attention from being trampled.

In Closing

Office rules are not bureaucracy. They are the quiet scaffolding that makes everything else possible. Without them, people default to chaos. With them, energy is directed to the work that matters.

The power of communication contracts, decision hygiene, and capacity boundaries is that they are simple, memorable, and scalable. A two-person startup can use them. A global corporation can too.

More importantly, they shift the culture from one of accidental overload to one of deliberate respect. When teams agree on how they will communicate, decide, and protect boundaries, they stop wasting cognitive capacity on noise. They start using it for creativity, strategy, and team performance.

These rules are not the whole solution. But they are the floor that makes higher-level capacity possible. Without them, even the best individual practices collapse. With them, workplaces become places where people can think, contribute, and thrive.

Ask Yourself:

- Which communication tool in my workplace creates the most confusion?
- What capacity language could help me decline without guilt?
- What's an example of a team rule I wish were written down but isn't?
- Who in my workplace models good boundaries— and what could I learn from them?
- If clarity is kindness, what's one way I could be kinder in my communication this week?

CHAPTER 13

ANTICIPATE

Uncertainty is the only certainty there is, and knowing how to live with insecurity is the only security.

—John Allen Paulos

Productivity is rarely a straight line. We sketch out neat pathways, picture smooth progress, and convince ourselves that the week will unfold exactly as planned. But reality doesn't work that way. Emails arrive uninvited. Meetings spill over. Children get sick. Markets wobble. Technology fails. Bad night's sleeps happen. Something unexpected always enters the frame.

This is where anticipation matters. Not as pessimism, but as preparation. Anticipation enhances your state of being proactive. It's about seeing ahead—not to control everything, but to avoid being caught flat-footed. Without anticipation, even the most carefully built system for cognitive capacity becomes brittle.

Anticipation has different connotations. Sometimes it feels negative: worry, overpreparing, rehearsing disasters in your head. Sometimes it feels positive: readiness, resilience, confidence. And sometimes, when absent, it leaves you exposed. Think of it like packing an umbrella. Most days you won't need it. But when the storm arrives, you're grateful it's there. The umbrella doesn't stop the rain—it stops you from being drenched.

NASA engineers embody this principle—anticipating the negative and turning it positive. Mission control teams spend months writing "failure scripts" before a launch: What if a booster fails? What if a sensor misreads? What if communication drops? They don't expect all these things to happen. But if one does, the team already knows its first move. Anticipation gives them clarity in chaos.

Why Anticipation Builds Capacity

Research in situational awareness, which we touched on earlier (Endsley, 1995), shows that anticipating deviations improves decision speed and reduces error. In other words, expectation sharpens performance. You can act more decisively when you have already sketched the likely paths ahead.

Studies on information foraging by Pirolli and Card (1999) echo this principle in the digital realm. They drew an analogy between how humans search for information and how animals forage for food. Just as animals follow "scent trails" toward the richest sources of nourishment, people rely on cues—headlines, hyperlinks, subject lines, folder names—to decide where to invest attention. When the scent is strong, search is efficient. When it is weak or misleading, we waste effort wandering, clicking, and backtracking. The cost of poor cues is high. Every dead end, irrelevant link, or misleading document is like searching in barren ground—it consumes time and drains energy without yielding results. And when new input arrives without warning, without your anticipation, it's like being startled mid-forage: focus is lost, and the brain must reorient before progress can continue. That reorientation is not free; it burns capacity.

The metaphor reveals why so many workplaces feel exhausting. Employees spend hours chasing information through poorly designed systems—multiple platforms, outdated repositories, endless email chains. The "information scent" is faint, which results in a prolonged search. Productivity plummets, not because workers lack skill, but because the environment is misaligned with how the brain naturally hunts for what it needs.

Preparedness preserves capacity. If the right work path and potential deviations are mapped out, the brain conserves energy, and attention is spent on analysis and action, not on endless searching. This doesn't mean anticipating every detail. It means building buffer zones into plans. It means practicing simple "if–then" scripts: When X happens, I'll do Y. It means having a container—let's call it the "unforeseen shit box"—for the unexpected, so surprises don't derail your entire system.

Anticipation is not a separate pillar of cognitive capacity. It's the mindset that runs through all three elements. Anticipation is the quiet discipline that acknowledges complexity without surrendering to it. It's building your deviation awareness. It doesn't eliminate uncertainty, but it turns uncertainty into something you can hold.

- **Criteria** become stronger when they account for disruption: you don't just decide what matters, you also decide what matters when things go wrong.
- **Chunking** becomes adaptive when you expect interruptions: you group work in ways that can flex and recover rather than shatter on impact.
- **Closure** becomes more sustainable when you allow for unfinishedness: you don't expect everything to tie up neatly, but you know how to close what matters even in messy conditions.

Look at your own week. How often did it follow the straight line you imagined on Monday morning? Probably never. But how often did you plan for that? You know disruptions will come. You know input will exceed expectations. You know the unforeseen will appear. So you design for it. You make peace with the curve instead of fighting for the impossible line.

That shift—from surprise to expectation—is the difference between feeling overwhelmed and feeling equipped.

Anticipation is the
quiet discipline that
acknowledges complexity
without surrendering to
it. It doesn't eliminate
uncertainty, but it
turns uncertainty into
something you can hold.

Action Steps:

1. **Anticipate disruptions**—build deviation awareness; ask "what could pull me off track?"
2. **Anticipate input**—expect emails, meetings, urgent requests, don't pretend they won't come.
3. **Anticipate the unforeseen** ("shit box")—have a container for the unexpected, so chaos doesn't derail your system.
4. **Reset expectations**—remember that productivity isn't a straight line. Build buffer zones into your plans.
5. **Rehearse first steps**—when X happens, I'll do Y. Clarity calms disruption.

In Closing

Cognitive capacity is not just about squeezing more productivity out of a crowded world. If that were the goal, we'd be no different from the productivity hacks and quick fixes that have littered bookshelves for decades. Instead, it's about building the mental space to live and work with clarity, calm, and resilience.

Anticipation ensures that this clarity survives impact. When you anticipate, you stop living at the mercy of surprises. You work with the confidence that, whatever comes, your system can absorb it. Anticipation is what keeps that clarity intact when reality doesn't match the plan. It's the shock absorber in the system, the element that allows Criteria, Chunking, and Closure to remain intact under pressure. Without it, the first disruption topples the structure. To anticipate is not to obsess over every possible failure. It is to accept that disruptions will come and to meet them with preparedness rather than panic.

When you operate this way, you stop being hostage to surprises. A derailed meeting, a sudden request, or a delayed project no longer destroys your sense of control. You respond, adjust, and move forward because you expected the unexpected. Your system doesn't shatter; it absorbs.

This is the true future of productivity. Not perfection. Not the fantasy of a life without interruptions. But preparedness—a way of working and living that acknowledges reality without being crushed by it. A future where we don't simply survive disruption, but navigate it effectively.

And perhaps, in that steadiness, there is a deeper kind of freedom: the freedom to trust that our capacity is enough, even when the world is not.

Ask Yourself:

- What "failure scripts" could I borrow from NASA in my own work?
- Where do I most often underestimate input—emails, meetings, requests?
- Do I have a "shit box"—a way to hold the unexpected without panic?
- How do I react emotionally when plans don't go to plan?
- How could anticipation make my work not just more productive, but more peaceful?

Epilogue

Thank you for reading, and more importantly, for pausing long enough to reflect on your own capacity. In a world that rewards speed, attention is an act of courage. By finishing this book, you've already proven that you are willing to carve out space for clarity.

What comes next is not about grand reinventions. It's about choosing, moment by moment, to notice how you work with your cognitive capacity. It's about setting rules that respect your time, creating buffers that absorb disruption, and learning to close loops so your mind can breathe again.

Put something in practice, reflect, adjust, and try again.

No one can remove the noise of the world. But each of us can choose how much of it we let in. And in that choice lies the possibility of workplaces that nurture focus, teams that communicate with respect, and lives that feel not just busy, but meaningful.

It's your responsibility to help your brain make more sense of the world, avoid overload, and through that, you become more productive. Work with your brain, not against it.

And remember: you're not failing, you're just overloaded. But you now have the tools to overcome this. It's up to you to use them.

Acknowledgements

A book is a significant endeavour for any person. But it's never a one-person job. I'm tremendously grateful to so many people. Most of you probably don't even realise you made a contribution to this book. You may have been an inspiration as you share your own challenges around information overload. You may have nudged me to write a second book, as the topic is so needed. You may have simply attended one of my workshop sessions, and just a little head nod would've made me realise there's more going on with our productivity challenge. Or you may have been another amazing expert in this field, and your work is part of the foundation I could build on.

To my editor, Johanna Leigh, for being willing to work with me again and doing a fabulous job yet again. Your care and attention to detail are wonderful. It's a pleasure working with you.

To my mentor, Jane Anderson, for being the system behind my chaos. You are incredible at streamlining and simplifying the complexities that come with running a thought leadership practice.

To my community of peers, colleagues, and friends—you are all amazing. Whether I met you at a networking function, an introduction, or just via LinkedIn, thank you for being on this journey with me. It's amazing having you in my corner, and I love that we get to support each other.

To my instructors and community of my martial arts organisation, World Moo Duk Kwan, you keep me inspired, motivated, and you fuel my determination. I am proud and privileged to be part of this family, of something bigger than me. Putting on my white karate uniform at the end of the day helps me with my own closure practice.

To my family, far away in the Netherlands, Mum, Dad, and my brother Martijn, I love you.

And, as for the one who is closest to me, who stands by my side every day, who cheers me on and challenges me at the same time, but who is most of all my biggest supporter in this all—my husband, Frank Akkerboom. Together, we make great decisions, and I love the life we are building.

Work With Eve

With over 15 years of experience as an environmental professional, Eve works with teams and leaders to effectively manage information overload to boost productivity and mental clarity in today's fast-paced work environments. With a double Master's Degree in environmental science and marine biology, Eve's scientific background enables her to analyse and resolve the impact of the complexity of our work environment on our productivity.

Her personal journey—from growing up in the Netherlands to living in remote Western Australia and now residing in Perth, Australia—has shaped her understanding of how our surroundings affect our mental capacity.

Eve typically helps:

- CEO's, HR Directors and GMs who want to support their team from feeling bombarded with emails, texts, social media, noise, requests, and expectations.
- Meeting planners and conference organisers looking for an insightful, fun and engaging speaker to speak on a unique area of productivity.
- Leaders who are overloaded, making it difficult to focus on what truly matters; to create the cognitive capacity that is required to do our best work.

Eve:

- Speaks passionately yet pragmatically on productivity, well-being and mental clarity.
- Facilitates engaging workshops on how to focus, reducing noise and streamlining your workflow.
- Coaches busy professionals to help manage time, energy and capacity.
- Provides programs for organisations which need a boost in performance to equip employees with a simpler approach.

Clients have included:
Rio Tinto, Red Bull, MNG, Glencore, Mission Australia

Outside her commitment to creating cognitive capacity, she's happy in her martial arts uniform (3rd degree black belt in Korean Karate and the National Chair), or quality time with her dog Cargo.

Email: info@evebroenland.com

Call: +61 400 201 361

More info: www.evebroenland.com

References

Chapter 1

Research & Theory

Baumeister, R. F., Bratslavsky, E., Muraven, M., & Tice, D. M. (1998). Ego depletion: Is the active self a limited resource? *Journal of Personality and Social Psychology, 74*(5), 1252–1265. https://doi.org/10.1037/0022-3514.74.5.1252

Fredrickson, B. L. (2001). The role of positive emotions in positive psychology: The broaden-and-build theory of positive emotions. *American Psychologist, 56*(3), 218–226. https://doi.org/10.1037/0003-066X.56.3.218

Kahneman, D., & Tversky, A. (1979). Prospect theory: An analysis of decision under risk. *Econometrica, 47*(2), 263–292. https://doi.org/10.2307/1914185

Leroy, S. (2009). Why is it so hard to do my work? The challenge of attention residue when switching between work tasks. *Organizational Behavior and Human Decision Processes, 109*(2), 168–181. https://doi.org/10.1016/j.obhdp.2009.04.002

Books

Gazzaley, A., & Rosen, L. D. (2016). *The distracted mind: Ancient brains in a high-tech world.* MIT Press.

Hari, J. (2022). *Stolen focus: Why you can't pay attention—and how to think deeply again.* Crown.

Levitin, D. J. (2014). *The organized mind: Thinking straight in the age of information overload.* Dutton.

Mullainathan, S., & Shafir, E. (2013). *Scarcity: Why having too little means so much.* Times Books.

Newport, C. (2016). *Deep work: Rules for focused success in a distracted world.* Grand Central Publishing.

Newport, C. (2021). *A world without email: Reimagining work in an age of communication overload.* Portfolio.

Chapter 2

Core Reports & Studies

Brosix. (2024, November 7). Digital communication overload: Statistics, effects, and how to manage it. Brosix.

Cottrill Research. (2023, March 24). Workers spend too much time searching for information. Cottrill Research.

Deloitte. (2021). *Workplace burnout survey*. Deloitte Insights.Financial Times. (2024, May 28). Ending the "infinite workday." *Financial Times*. https://www.ft.com/content/9ac508d5-5df1-4f78-873e-c6edf2d2abf9

Financial Times. (2024, July 16). The human mind is in a recession. *Financial Times*. https://www.ft.com/content/c288abc6-24a4-4062-aeb4-05c463ae7289

Gallup. (2023). *State of the global workplace*. Gallup, Inc.

IT Pro. (2025, February 11). 'Always on' culture is harming productivity, so workers are demanding "digital silence" to get on with tasks. *IT Pro*.

https://www.itpro.com/business/business-strategy/always-on-culture-is-harming-productivity-so-workers-are-demanding-digital-silence-to-get-on-with-tasks

Microsoft. (2021–2023). *Work trend index reports*. Microsoft.

StudyFinds. (2023, February 24). Overloaded! 83% of workers feel overwhelmed by the amount of information they must process. *StudyFinds*.

Twilio Segment. (2025). *The digital worker experience report 2025*. Twilio.

Wikipedia contributors. (2025, August 23). Continuous partial attention. In *Wikipedia*. https://en.wikipedia.org/wiki/Continuous_partial_attention

Wikipedia contributors. (2025, August 23). Infomania. In *Wikipedia*. https://en.wikipedia.org/wiki/Infomania

Wikipedia contributors. (2025, August 23). Technostress. In *Wikipedia*.

World Health Organization. (2019). Burn-out an "occupational phenomenon": International classification of diseases. WHO.

Research & Theory

Endsley, M. R. (1995). Toward a theory of situation awareness in dynamic systems. *Human Factors, 37*(1), 32–64. https://doi.org/10.1518/001872095779049543

Mark, G., Voida, S., & Cardello, A. (2012). A pace not dictated by electrons: An empirical study of work without email. *Proceedings of the SIGCHI Conference on Human Factors in Computing Systems* (pp. 555–564). https://doi.org/10.1145/2207676.2207754

Miller, G. A. (1956). The magical number seven, plus or minus two: Some limits on our capacity for processing information. *Psychological Review, 63*(2), 81–97. https://doi.org/10.1037/h0043158

Simon, H. A. (1971). Designing organizations for an information-rich world. In M. Greenberger (Ed.), *Computers, communications, and the public interest* (pp. 37–72). Johns Hopkins University Press.

Books

Baumeister, R. F., & Tierney, J. (2011). *Willpower: Rediscovering the greatest human strength.* Penguin Press.

Harris, T. (2020). *The Social Dilemma* [Film]. Exposure Labs.

Chapter 3

Research & Theory

Mark, G. (2004–2023). UC Irvine studies on interruptions and task switching. [Multiple works].

Chapter 4

Research & Theory

Baumeister, R. F., Bratslavsky, E., Muraven, M., & Tice, D. M. (1998). Ego depletion: Is the active self a limited resource? *Journal of Personality and Social Psychology, 74*(5), 1252–1265. https://doi.org/10.1037/0022-3514.74.5.1252

Baumeister, R. F., & Bushman, B. J. (2014). *Social psychology and human nature* (3rd ed.). Cengage Learning. [Contains a concise summary of the Zeigarnik effect].

Iyengar, S. S., & Lepper, M. R. (2000). When choice is demotivating: Can one desire too much of a good thing? *Journal of Personality and Social Psychology, 79*(6), 995–1006. https://doi.org/10.1037/0022-3514.79.6.995

Ryan, R. M., & Deci, E. L. (2000). Self-determination theory and the facilitation of intrinsic motivation, social development, and well-being. *American Psychologist, 55*(1), 68–78. https://doi.org/10.1037/0003-066X.55.1.68

Sweller, J. (1988). Cognitive load during problem solving: Effects on learning. *Cognitive Science, 12*(2), 257–285. https://doi.org/10.1207/s15516709cog1202_4

Zeigarnik, B. (1927). Das Behalten erledigter und unerledigter Handlungen. *Psychologische Forschung, 9*(1), 1–85. https://doi.org/10.1007/BF02409755

Books

Schwartz, B. (2004). *The paradox of choice: Why more is less.* Harper Perennial.

Chapter 5

Research & Theory

Endsley, M. R. (1995). Toward a theory of situation awareness in dynamic systems. *Human Factors, 37*(1), 32–64. https://doi.org/10.1518/001872095779049543

Simons, D. J., & Chabris, C. F. (1999). Gorillas in our midst: Sustained inattentional blindness for dynamic events. *Perception, 28*(9), 1059–1074. https://doi.org/10.1068/p281059

Books

Chabris, C. F., & Simons, D. J. (2010). *The invisible gorilla: How our intuitions deceive us.* Crown.

Endsley, M. R. (2016). *Designing for situation awareness: An approach to user-centered design* (2nd ed.). CRC Press. https://doi.org/10.1201/9781315605685

Wilson, T. D. (2002). *Strangers to ourselves: Discovering the adaptive unconscious.* Harvard University Press.

Chapter 6

Core Reports & Studies

RescueTime. (2019, February 13). *How much time do we spend on email?.* RescueTime Blog. https://blog.rescuetime.com/email-and-distraction

Research & Theory

Brody, L. R., & Hall, J. A. (2008). Gender and emotion in context. In M. Lewis, J. M. Haviland-Jones, & L. F. Barrett (Eds.), *Handbook of emotions* (3rd ed., pp. 395–408). Guilford Press.

Frost, R. O., & Hartl, T. L. (1996). A cognitive–behavioral model of compulsive hoarding. *Behaviour Research and Therapy, 34*(4), 341–350. https://doi.org/10.1016/0005-7967(95)00071-2

Leroy, S. (2009). Why is it so hard to do my work? The challenge of attention residue when switching between work tasks. *Organizational Behavior and Human Decision Processes, 109*(2), 168–181. https://doi.org/10.1016/j.obhdp.2009.04.002

Lieberman, M. D., Eisenberger, N. I., Crockett, M. J., Tom, S. M., Pfeifer, J. H., & Way, B. M. (2007). Putting feelings into words: Affect labeling disrupts amygdala activity in response to affective stimuli. *Psychological Science, 18*(5), 421–428. https://doi.org/10.1111/j.1467-9280.2007.01916.x

Mark, G. (2004–2023). UC Irvine studies on interruptions and task switching. [Multiple works].

Meyer, D. E., & Schvaneveldt, R. W. (1971). Facilitation in recognizing pairs of words: Evidence of a dependence between retrieval operations. *Journal of Experimental Psychology, 90*(2), 227–234. https://doi.org/10.1037/h0031564

Miller, G. A. (1956). The magical number seven, plus or minus two: Some limits on our capacity for processing information. *Psychological Review, 63*(2), 81–97. https://doi.org/10.1037/h0043158

Roberson, D., Davies, I. R. L., & Davidoff, J. (2000). Color categories are not universal: Replications and new evidence from a stone-age culture. *Journal of Experimental Psychology: General, 129*(3), 369–398. https://doi.org/10.1037/0096-3445.129.3.369

Books

Barrett, L. F. (2017). *How emotions are made: The secret life of the brain.* Houghton Mifflin Harcourt.

Gazzaley, A., & Rosen, L. D. (2016). *The distracted mind.* MIT Press.

Hari, J. (2022). *Stolen focus.* Crown.

Lakoff, G. (2004). *Don't think of an elephant!: Know your values and frame the debate.* Chelsea Green Publishing.

Levitin, D. J. (2014). *The organized mind.* Dutton.

Mullainathan, S., & Shafir, E. (2013). *Scarcity: The new science of having less and how it defines our lives*. Times Books.

Newport, C. (2021). *A world without email: Reimagining work in an age of communication overload*. Portfolio.

Paulos, J. A. (1999). *Once upon a number: The hidden mathematical logic of stories*. Basic Books.

Chapter 7

Research & Theory

Baumeister, R. F., & Bushman, B. J. (2014). *Social psychology and human nature* (3rd ed.). Cengage Learning. [Contains a concise summary of the Zeigarnik effect].

Leroy, S. (2009). Why is it so hard to do my work? The challenge of attention residue when switching between work tasks. *Organizational Behavior and Human Decision Processes, 109*(2), 168–181. https://doi.org/10.1016/j.obhdp.2009.04.002

Books

Allen, D. (2001). *Getting things done: The art of stress-free productivity*. Viking.

Headlee, C. (2020). *Do nothing*. Harmony.

Newport, C. (2016). *Deep work*. Grand Central Publishing.

Odell, J. (2019). *How to do nothing*. Melville House.

Pang, A. S.-K. (2016). *Rest: Why you get more done when you work less*. Basic Books.

Chapter 8

Research & Theory

Grant, A. M. (2008). The significance of task significance: Job performance effects, relational mechanisms, and boundary conditions. *Journal of Applied Psychology, 93*(1), 108–124. https://doi.org/10.1037/0021-9010.93.1.108

Simon, H. A. (1956). Rational choice and the structure of the environment. *Psychological Review, 63*(2), 129–138. https://doi.org/10.1037/h0042769

Books

Adams, W., & Myles, T. (2020). *Meaningful work: A practical guide to leading extraordinary teams*. HarperCollins Leadership.

Allen, D. (2001). *Getting things done*. Viking.

Duke, A. (2020). *How to decide: Simple tools for making better choices.* Portfolio/Penguin.

Frei, F., & Morriss, A. (2020). *Unleashed: The unapologetic leader's guide to empowering everyone around you.* Harvard Business Review Press.

Mullainathan, S., & Shafir, E. (2013). *Scarcity: The new science of having less and how it defines our lives.* Times Books.

Kahneman, D. (2011). *Thinking, fast and slow.* Farrar, Straus and Giroux.

Schwartz, B. (2004). *The paradox of choice: Why more is less.* Harper Perennial.

Chapter 9

Research & Theory

Mark, G. (2004–2023). UC Irvine studies on interruptions and task switching. [Multiple works].

Books

Allen, D. (2001). *Getting things done.* Viking.

Mark, G. (2023). *Attention span: A groundbreaking way to restore balance, happiness, and productivity.* Hanover Square Press.

Newport, C. (2021). *A world without email: Reimagining work in an age of communication overload.* Portfolio.

Pang, A. S.-K. (2016). *Rest: Why you get more done when you work less.* Basic Books.

Chapter 10

Research & Theory

Altmann, E. M., & Trafton, J. G. (2002). Memory for goals: An activation-based model. *Cognitive Science, 26*(1), 39–83. https://doi.org/10.1207/s15516709cog2601_2

Einstein, G. O., & McDaniel, M. A. (1990). Normal aging and prospective memory. *Journal of Experimental Psychology: Learning, Memory, and Cognition, 16*(4), 717–726. https://doi.org/10.1037/0278-7393.16.4.717

Risko, E. F., & Gilbert, S. J. (2016). Cognitive offloading. *Trends in Cognitive Sciences, 20*(9), 676–688. https://doi.org/10.1016/j.tics.2016.07.002

Sonnentag, S., & Fritz, C. (2015). Recovery from job stress: The stressor-detachment model as an integrative framework. *Journal of Organizational Behavior, 36*(S1), S72–S103. https://doi.org/10.1002/job.1924

Books

Gawande, A. (2009). *The checklist manifesto: How to get things right.* Metropolitan Books.

Headlee, C. (2020). *Do nothing: How to break away from overworking, overdoing, and underliving.* Harmony.

Hutchins, E. (1995). *Cognition in the wild.* MIT Press.

Chapter 13

Research & Theory

Endsley, M. R. (1995). Toward a theory of situation awareness. *Human Factors, 37*(1), 32–64. https://doi.org/10.1518/001872095779049543

Pirolli, P., & Card, S. (1999). Information foraging. *Psychological Review, 106*(4), 643–675. https://doi.org/10.1037/0033-295X.106.4.643

www.ingramcontent.com/pod-product-compliance
Lightning Source LLC
Chambersburg PA
CBHW050025040726
47599CB00015B/1543